T0318399

"Gantt and Williams's edited volume brings together a stellar cast of contributors, all of whom seek to show, in their own distinctive ways, that the reigning, largely 'scientistic,' view of psychological inquiry is but one view among many possible ones. By alerting us to the parochial nature of the dominant view, they pave the way toward fashioning not only a broader, more inclusive perspective on what psychological inquiry might be but a vastly expanded, more humanly adequate, vision of the discipline itself."

Mark Freeman, Distinguished Professor of Ethics and
Society, College of the Holy Cross, USA

On Hijacking Science

This book examines the origins, presence, and implications of scientistic thinking in psychology. Scientism embodies the claim that only knowledge attained by means of natural scientific methods counts as valid and valuable. This perspective increasingly dominates thinking and practice in psychology and is seldom acknowledged as anything other than standard scientific practice. This book seeks to make this intellectual movement explicit and to detail the very real limits in both role and reach of science in psychology. The critical chapters in this volume present an alternative perspective to the scholarly mainstreams of the discipline and will be of value to scholars and students interested in the scientific status and the philosophical bases of psychology as a discipline.

Edwin E. Gantt is Associate Professor of Psychology, Brigham Young University. He has formal training in phenomenology and hermeneutics, and has published broadly in the theory and philosophy of psychology.

Richard N. Williams is Professor of Psychology and Director of the Wheatley Institution, Brigham Young University. He has published on topics related to scientism, human agency, and theoretical psychology.

Advances in Theoretical and Philosophical Psychology
Series Editor
Brent D. Slife
Brigham Young University

The Hidden Worldviews of Psychology's Theory, Research, and Practice
Brent D. Slife, Kari A. O'Grady, and Russell D. Kosits

On Hijacking Science
Exploring the Nature and Consequences of Overreach in Psychology
Edwin E. Gantt and Richard N. Williams

www.routledge.com/psychology/series/TPP

On Hijacking Science

Exploring the Nature and Consequences of Overreach in Psychology

Edited by Edwin E. Gantt and Richard N. Williams

Routledge
Taylor & Francis Group

LONDON AND NEW YORK

First published 2018 by Routledge

2 Park Square, Milton Park, Abingdon, Oxfordshire OX14 4RN

52 Vanderbilt Avenue, New York, NY 10017

Routledge is an imprint of the Taylor & Francis Group, an informa business

First issued in paperback 2019

Library of Congress Cataloging-in-Publication Data
Names: Gantt, Edwin E., 1965– editor. | Williams, Richard N., 1950– editor.
Title: On hijacking science : exploring the nature and consequences of
    overreach in psychology/edited by Edwin E. Gantt and Richard N. Williams.
Description: New York, NY : Routledge, 2018. | Series: Advances in
    theoretical and philosophical psychology | Includes bibliographical
references and index.
Identifiers: LCCN 2018003034 | ISBN 9781138478817 (hardback : alk. paper)
    ISBN 9781351062572 (ebook : alk. paper)
Subjects: LCSH: Psychology—Philosophy. | Psychology—Study and teaching.
Classification: LCC BF38. O596 2018 | DDC 150.1—dc23
LC record available at https://lccn.loc.gov/2018003034

ISBN 13: 978-1-138-47881-7 (hbk)
ISBN 13: 978-0-367-85614-4 (pbk)

Typeset in Times New Roman by
Apex CoVantage, LLC

To my wonderful, bouncy, beautiful grandson, Easton Callan Gantt. Learn all there is to learn, both in heaven and earth, love even those who are hardest to love, and never, ever be fooled by nonsense, no matter how fashionable.

—Edwin E. Gantt

To DNR in *teleia philia*.

—Richard N. Williams

Contents

Contributors

Sheilagh T. Fox is a doctoral candidate in the Clinical Psychology program at Brigham Young University. Her research interests include theoretical and health psychology.

Edwin E. Gantt is an Associate Professor in the Department of Psychology at Brigham Young University. He received his doctorate in clinical psychology from Duquesne University in Pittsburgh, Pennsylvania, where he studied existential, phenomenological, and hermeneutic approaches to psychological theory. Currently, his research interests include philosophy of social science, psychology of religion, and the problematic conceptual and practical implications that neo-Darwinian theory and scientism have for any psychology seeking to offer meaningful accounts of moral agency, altruism, and religious experience. He has authored over 60 scholarly articles in these and similar areas, and has co-edited the books *Psychology-for-the-Other: Levinas, Ethics, and the Practice of Psychology* (with Richard N. Williams) and *Taking Sides: Clashing Views on Psychological Issues* (with Brent D. Slife). He is currently an associate editor at the *Journal of Theoretical and Philosophical Psychology* and *Issues in Religion and Psychotherapy*.

Eric A. Ghelfi is a doctoral candidate in the Clinical Psychology program at Brigham Young University. His research interests include philosophy of social science and issues surrounding replication in psychology.

James T. Lamiell is Professor of Psychology, Emeritus, Georgetown University. His scholarly interests are in the history, philosophy, and research methods of psychology. All three of these areas of interest are served by his continuing engagement with the works of the German philosopher and psychologist William Stern (1871–1938). He is the author of numerous peer-reviewed articles in prestigious scholarly journals, and is also the author of *The Psychology of Personality: An Epistemological Inquiry*, *Beyond Individual and Group Differences: Human Individuality, Scientific*

Psychology, and William Stern's Critical Personalism, and *William Stern (1871–1938): A Brief Introduction to His Life and Works.*

Lisa M. Osbeck is Professor of Psychology at the University of West Georgia and a Research Affiliate of the Georgia Institute of Technology. She is a Fellow of the Center for Philosophy of Science, University of Pittsburgh, and the American Psychological Association. She is the recipient of the Sigmund Koch Award (2005) and the Theodore Sarbin Award (2012) from the Society for Theoretical and Philosophical Psychology. Her co-authored book *Science as Psychology: Sense Making and Identity in Science Practice* (with Nancy J. Nersessian) was co-winner of the William James Book Award from the American Psychological Association (Division 1). She is the author and co-author of numerous scholarly papers, as well as the book *Rational Intuition: Philosophical Roots, Scientific Investigations* (with Barbara S. Held).

Jeffrey S. Reber is an Associate Professor and Chair of the Department of Psychology at University of West Georgia. His PhD is in general psychology with a dual emphasis in theoretical/philosophical psychology and applied social psychology. His research and teaching philosophies are informed by a relational approach to psychology that promotes critical thinking about the relationship between assumptions, implications, and alternative perspectives as they impact human sociality and consciousness. He has published 20 peer-reviewed journal articles, 10 book chapters, and two books that exemplify his relational, critical thinking approach to psychology. He also sits on the editorial boards of four academic peer review publication outlets and served as the president of the Society for Theoretical and Philosophical Psychology (Division 24 of the APA) in 2014.

Daniel N. Robinson is a former Associate Member and Fellow of the Faculty of Philosophy, University of Oxford. His published work covers a range of issues in neuroscience, intellectual history, philosophy of mind, and philosophy of law. He is the author of numerous peer-reviewed journal articles, as well as highly regarded books such as *Philosophy of Psychology, Aristotle's Psychology, An Intellectual History of Psychology, Wild Beasts and Idle Humours: The Insanity Defense From Antiquity to the Present, Consciousness and Mental Life,* and *How Is Nature Possible? Kant's Project in the First Critique.*

Brent D. Slife is Professor of Psychology and Richard L. Evans Chair of Religious Understanding at Brigham Young University. As the editor in chief of the *Journal of Theoretical and Philosophical Psychology,* his research interests include the conceptual underpinnings of psychotherapy, the philosophy of social science, and the interface between religion and psychology. Professor Slife has authored, co-authored, or edited numerous scholarly journal articles, book chapters, and books, including *Time and Psychological Explanation, What's Behind the Research? Discovering Hidden Assumptions in the Behavioral Sciences* (with Richard N. Williams), *Critical Thinking About Psychology: Hidden Assumptions and Plausible Alternatives* (with Jeffrey S. Reber and Frank C. Richardson), *Critical Issues in Psychotherapy: Translating New Ideas Into Practice* (with Richard N. Williams and Sally H. Barlow), *Frailty, Suffering, and Vice: Flourishing in the Face of Human Limitations* (with Blaine J. Fowers and Frank C. Richardson), and *The Hidden Worlds of Psychology's Theory, Research, and Practice* (with Kari O'Grady and Russell D. Kostis).

Frederick J. Wertz is Professor of Psychology at Fordham University and has written extensively on philosophy, theory, methodology, and the history of psychology. He is the co-author of *Five Ways of Doing Qualitative Analysis: Phenomenological Psychology, Grounded Theory, Discourse Analysis, Narrative Research, and Intuitive Inquiry*. He is former editor of the *Journal of Phenomenological Psychology* and the *Bulletin of Theoretical and Philosophical Psychology*. He is also former president of Divisions 24 (Theory and Philosophy) and 32 (Humanistic Psychology) of the American Psychological Association, and of the Interdisciplinary Coalition of North American Phenomenologists. Professor Wertz is a Rollo May Awardee (2014) in the APA Society for Humanistic Psychology and current president of the APA Society for Qualitative Inquiry in Psychology.

Richard N. Williams is founding Director of the Wheatley Institution at Brigham Young University, serving since 2007. From 2001 to 2008, he served as an Associate Academic Vice President for Faculty at BYU. He is a Professor in the Department of Psychology at BYU where he began teaching in 1981. His specialty areas include the philosophical, theoretical, and historical foundations of psychology, with a special concentration on issues related to human agency, as well the science of psychology and research methods and statistics. Professor Williams has authored, co-authored, or edited numerous journal articles and books, including *Reconsidering Psychology: Perspectives From Continental Philosophy* (with James E. Faulconer), *Psychology-for-the-Other: Levinas, Ethics, and the Practice of Psychology* (with Edwin E. Gantt), *What's Behind the Research? Discovering Hidden Assumptions in the Behavioral Sciences* (with Brent D. Slife), and *Scientism: The New Orthodoxy* (with Daniel N. Robinson).

Series Editor's Foreword

Psychologists need to face the facts. Their commitment to empiricism for answering disciplinary questions does not prevent pivotal questions from arising that cannot be evaluated empirically, hence the title of this series: *Advances in Theoretical and Philosophical Psychology*. Such questions as: What is the relation between mind and body? What is the nature of a good life? And even: Are current psychological methods adequate to truly understand the person? These questions are in some sense philosophical, to be sure, but the discipline of psychology cannot advance even its own empirical agenda without addressing questions like these in defensible ways. Indeed, it could be argued that there is no empirical evidence for the epistemology of empiricism itself!

How then does the discipline of psychology deal with such nonempirical questions? We could leave the answers exclusively to professional philosophers, but this would mean that the conceptual foundations of the discipline, including the conceptual framework of empiricism itself, is left to scholars who are *outside* the discipline. As undoubtedly helpful as philosophers are and will be, this situation would mean that the people doing the actual psychological work, psychologists themselves, are divorced from the people who formulate and reformulate the conceptual foundations of that work. This division of labor would seem dangerous to the long-term viability of the discipline.

Instead, the founders of psychology—thinkers such as Wundt, Freud, and James—recognized the importance of psychologists themselves in formulating their own foundations. These parents of psychology not only did their own theorizing, in cooperation with many others; they realized the significance of constantly reexamining these theories and philosophies, including the theories and philosophies of psychology's methods. The people most involved in the discipline's activities would thus be the ones most knowledgeable about whether and how such changes needed to be made. This series is dedicated to the examining and reexamining of these foundations.

The present book is a vital part of this historic project. It recognizes that our conception of science is itself a conception, not a step-by-step recipe for knowledge, but a philosophy of how knowledge is advanced. Indeed, one of the freedoms of scientists is that they are not relegated to one particular philosophy of knowledge acquisition. As the noted historian of science, Paul Feyerabend (1995), put it: "science is not one thing; it is many; it is not closed, but open to new approaches" (p. 809). The present book investigates the often-unwitting reification of a specific philosophical conception of science in psychology—that only knowledge gathered through the careful application of certifiably natural science methods can count as valid and valuable knowledge. Indeed, this book demonstrates how scientism has often become the unacknowledged norm of psychological research. It not only identifies the problems of scientism in psychology; it also explores the possibility of alternative conceptions of psychological research and practice.

Brent D. Slife

Reference

Feyerabend, P. (1995). History of the philosophy of science. In T. Honderich (ed.), *Oxford Companion to Philosophy* (pp. 806-809). Oxford, UK: Oxford University Press.

Preface: A 'Science' of Psychology: The Enduring Aspiration

As early as 1600 BC, we find in the *Smith Papyrus* the various stages of medical investigations into the nature and causes of illness and death: clinical examination, various treatment modalities, short- and long-term prognosis (Breasted, 1991). The record of systematic observation, inductive reasoning, prediction and control is, indeed, a long and successful one. Why then does psychology still struggle to define itself?

Toward the conclusion of his *Critique of Pure Reason*, Kant (2003) considers the prospects for a scientific psychology. Having established that reason alone cannot vindicate claims regarding the unity, immateriality, and immortality of the 'soul' or mental substance, he wonders whether some other means might not be found. Failing in this, he offers temporary safe harbor:

> Though it is but a stranger it has long been accepted as a member of the household, and we allow it to stay for some time longer, until it is in a position to set up an establishment of its own.
>
> (p. 664)

Attempts to set up an establishment of its own mark a cluttered and frustrating history. Correlative studies based on neurological and neurosurgical findings never did (and never could) yield an independent science, but a clearly *dependent* one. Freud's famous *Project* was explicitly 'neuronal' and required acceptance of psychoanalytic theory if one were to test its validity (see, Freud, 1950; Robinson, 2016). Behaviorism—in the thrall of a form of positivism—oscillated between the denial of the 'mental' and a less than credible translation algorithm permitting one to use bar-presses and turns in mazes as indicators of cognitive processes. These are all twice-told tales by now, less examples of failure than, perhaps, of simply missing the point. And the point? There is no single, settled model of science itself, nor is it obvious that a given set of issues or problems will be settled by methodological resources borrowed from disciplines in which such issues and problems never arise. Saline does not suffer from depression and quarks are never angry, full stop. Newton did not consult but created methods of analysis. His ardent attachment to alchemy never found him confusing the principles at work in that realm with those associated with optical or gravitational phenomena. He adopted a foundational 'corpuscularian' ontology but not at the expense of taking phenomena where and as they are found and then attempting to discern such lawful relationships that might allow explanation and prediction. The same can be said of Galileo, Boyle, Hooke, and that entire school of students of nature.

In his *Two New Sciences*, Galileo tests older ("Aristotelian") explanations by applying mathematical analysis and something of a hypothetico-deductive model. But the mathematics and the model are chosen in light of the actual phenomena and not vice versa. Questions regarding the strength of various materials or rates of descent in a vacuum call for methods and models that are, as it were, independent of the psychological states of the observer. At least nothing in Galileo's (1914) account finds it necessary to consider them. Perhaps nothing in these very states requires or is illuminated by the methods and models found to be right for studies of tensile strength.

Newton (1999) reduced his own approach to what he offered as four rules for the mission of natural philosophy, his *Regulae Philosophandi*. In summary:

1. Admit no more causes than such as are both true and sufficient to explain a phenomenon.
2. Assign the same causes to the same effects.
3. Such qualities of bodies, which admit neither intension nor remission of degrees, and which are found to belong to all bodies within the reach of our experiments, are to be esteemed the universal qualities of all bodies whatsoever.
4. Look upon propositions collected by general induction from phenomena as accurately or very nearly true, notwithstanding any contrary hypotheses that may be imagined, until such time as other phenomena occur, by which they may either be made more accurate, or liable to exceptions.

(p. 795)

There is an anticipation here of that pragmatic theory so systematically developed by Charles Sanders Peirce. In "How to Make Our Ideas Clear" (1878), Peirce offers a picture of truth itself arising from an indefinitely long series of successful experiments. He puts it this way:

Our perversity and that of others may indefinitely postpone the settlement of opinion; it might even conceivably cause an arbitrary proposition to be universally accepted as long as the human race should last. Yet even that would not change the nature of the belief, which alone could be the result of investigation carried sufficiently far; and if, after the extinction of our race, another should arise with faculties and disposition for investigation, that true opinion must be the one which they would ultimately come to.

(p. 301)

Peirce illustrates this point more specifically and instructively. Quoting him at length:

One man may investigate the velocity of light by studying the transits of Venus and the aberration of the stars; another by the oppositions of Mars and the eclipses of Jupiter's satellites; a third by the method of Fizeau; a fourth by that of Foucault; a fifth by the motions of the curves of Lissajoux; a sixth, a seventh, an eighth, and a ninth, may follow the different methods of comparing the measures of statical and dynamical electricity. They may at first obtain different results, but, as each perfects his method and his processes, the results are found to move steadily together toward a destined centre. So with all scientific research. Different minds may set out with the most antagonistic views, but the progress of investigation carries them by a force outside of themselves to one and the same conclusion. This activity of thought by which we are carried, not where we wish, but to a foreordained goal, is like the operation of destiny. No modification of the point of view taken, no selection of other facts for study, no natural bent of mind even, can enable a man to escape the predestinate opinion. This great hope is embodied in the conception of truth and reality. The opinion which is fated to be ultimately agreed to by all who investigate, is what we mean by the truth, and the object represented in this opinion is the real. That is the way I would explain reality.

(p. 300)

If this rationale, along with Newton's strictures, is applied to psychology, we begin with that most basic canon: *Save the phenomenon*! One does not begin with a slavish attachment to a method whose very nature rules out essential features of reality. One cannot begin to think about the velocity of light but with light itself removed from reality! Nor can velocity or some measure of transit time be reduced to opinion or unshared beliefs. Aristotle teaches that every form of human grouping is formed with some end in view. This is a factual claim and can be assessed as such. But no assessment is needed to determine whether human forms of life are found in groups, from relatively unpopulous tribes to whole empires. What 'ends' account for participation? Are these shared ends or are they imposed? May there be an end, although members of the group are unaware of it—as in the beehive? Are such questions answered by noting a relationship between activity within the group and neural activity as visualized by functional magnetic resonance imaging (fMRI)? More generally, can one adopt a reductive strategy and still *save the phenomenon*?

Then, too, there are less global concerns that may prove to be sources of confusion and misdirection. Statistical treatments typically depersonalize phenomena that, by their very nature, presuppose the *person*. Repeated samples of light passed through graded filters can be averaged without fear, for one photon is like every other when it comes to the velocity of light. Five 'subjects' faced with the trolley problem may all choose not to cause a single death even though their decision will result in a dozen being struck by the unmanned trolley. But one may choose this on utilitarian grounds, another as a Kantian, a third committed to perfectionism, a fourth who simply doesn't care, and a fifth who flipped a coin and left the decision to chance. If the project is concerned with 'moral reasoning', a mere tally of yes–no votes is useless. And if it is *moral* reasoning that is at issue, the investigator has some responsibility for identifying just what it is that renders a decision 'moral'. The point, of course, is that statistics is not a mode of quantification and, in psychology, has a tendency to present data sets as if they were persons.

At any given point in the arc of its history, psychology has hosted promising approaches that finally ended nowhere (e.g., physiognomy, phrenology), in worrisome places (e.g., eugenics), or on a conceptual Ferris wheel (e.g., behaviorism). There is a 'cultural psychology' that rarely considers the nature and preconditions of culture itself; a psychology directed by a 'linguistic turn' that would have much of lived life patterned after a conversation; a psychology of 'lifespan development' that reports some of what changes between childhood and old age. Textbooks are produced in great numbers and journal articles stand as evidence of originality and passports to tenure. Nonetheless, the eager student who asks simply, "Just what is psychology about?" finds no clear answer widely adopted by the high priests of the discipline. Indeed, the subject was well understood in the 4th century BC when Aristotle classified the various 'psychic' powers and then came to terms with that special creature fit for the rule of law, attracted to a political form of life, and able to find fulfillment only by way of a perfectionist ideal with virtue as its end; all this, along with narrower reflections on learning and memory, dreaming, rhetoric, the emotions, gender differences—you get the picture. How odd that the only fully systematic psychology was the first one and that the coherence has been unraveling ever since.

The present volume offers neither panacea nor nosology. The contributions are modest, asking of readers only that much time to reflect on issues and possibilities not featured in textbooks or highlighted in *Psychology Today*. The summons is a call for clarity, even transparency when presenting to the wider world findings and theories allegedly bearing on nothing less than conscious, purposive life. In a domain rich in books that are, as it were, 'thick but thin', one may find appealing a volume that is 'thin but thick'.

Daniel N. Robinson

References

Breasted, J. H. (1991). *The Edwin Smith Surgical Papyrus: Published in facsimile and hieroglyphic transliteration and commentary in two volumes*. Chicago, IL: University of Chicago Oriental Institute. (Original work published 1931)

Freud, S. (1950). *Project for a scientific psychology*. In J. Strachey & A. Freud (Eds.), *The standard edition of the complete psychological works of Sigmund Freud: Pre-psycho-analytic publications and unpublished drafts* (Vol. 1, pp. 281–391). London: Hogarth Press. (Original work published 1895)

Galileo, G. (1914). *Dialogues concerning two new sciences* (H. Crew & A. de Salvio, Trans.). New York: Palgrave Macmillan.

Kant, I. (2003). *Critique of pure reason* (N. K. Smith, Trans.). New York: Palgrave Macmillan. (Original work published 1787)

Newton, I. (1999). *Philosophiae Naturalis Principia Mathematica* (I. B. Cohen & A. Whitman, Trans.). Oakland: University of California Press. (Original work published 1687)

Peirce, C. S. (1878, January). How to make our ideas clear. *Popular Science Monthly*, *12*, 286–302. Retrieved from http://courses.media.mit.edu/2004spring/mas966/Peirce%201878%20Make%20Ideas%20Clear.pdf

Robinson, D. N. (2016). Explanation and the "brain sciences". *Theory & Psychology*, *26*(3), 324–332.

Introduction: Science, Scientism, and Psychology

Richard N. Williams and Edwin E. Gantt

The interwar period of the 20th century provided the setting and context for a significant disturbance in the intellectual life of Europe (Sharpe, Jeffs, & Reynolds, 2017). The nature and source of this disturbance is captured in the title of the last book written, but not finished, by the German phenomenologist Edmund Husserl between 1934 and 1937, *The Crisis of European Sciences and Transcendental Phenomenology* (hereinafter the *Crisis*). It is clear from the title of this work Husserl intended to establish his work, transcendental phenomenology, as the foundation of an alternative to the prevailing *Wissenschaften*[1] that he, and a great many others, felt was responsible for the eruption and horror of World War I, as well as the intellectual and moral malaise pervading Europe (and especially Germany) at the time. As philosopher and intellectual historian, Petra Brown (2017) has observed:

> Facing sustained periods of political and social upheaval, the Neo-Kantian intelligentsia were challenged by a new generation of scholars who no longer believed in the internal order of their Neo-Kantian philosophy in the face of a disordered world. For the younger sons, the idolatry of reason of their elders had led Germany to a situation where the traditional tools of the *Wissenschaften* would prove ineffectual, and the Enlightenment ideal of progressive self-liberation was no longer believed to lead to true freedom. Reason's self-legislating and regulative functions seemed ill-equipped to confront the existential reality of a world 'in crisis'.

Husserl, and a great many other scholars, felt strongly the need for a reconfiguration of thinking that could suitably respond to the apparent failures of rationality, normative authority, intellectual and cultural progressivist narratives, nationalism, and imperialism (Jeffs & Sharpe, 2017, p. 7).

It is understandable that the crisis Husserl and so many others were so concerned about had occurred in Europe. Europe is, after all, the continent of the Enlightenment (Gay, 1977a, 1977b). The seeds of the Enlightenment (and subsequently the modern world) had been planted in the intellectual soil of ancient Greece, and the history of Western thought is the history of the cultivation and development of those seeds of metaphysics, epistemology, and ethics (Herman, 2013). The fruits of those vibrant seeds quickly matured and were harvested throughout Europe—and from there were spread to the rest of the world.

It must be acknowledged that much of the fruit of the Enlightenment has been quite good (Stark, 2014). After all, who would seriously bemoan the progress that has resulted in our conquering so many of the diseases that have ravaged humankind for centuries, increased supplies of food worldwide, provided far higher standards of living for millions, made education increasingly accessible, and produced technologies that have eased the burdens of life and made so many wonderful things possible that would otherwise not be available? We suspect that most who might bemoan these developments are probably more concerned about the 'howness' of their achievement, and the equity of distribution of their benefits, as well as the often less than careful attention to unintended consequences that accompanied them, rather than the actual advances themselves. It seems reasonable to assume, then, that on many if not most fronts (e.g., technological, political, medical, economic, and scientific), there are genuinely few people who would elect to return to life in premodern, pre-Enlightenment times.

However, in spite of all this, the crisis was real, as have been its effects. In the heading for Section 2 of Part I of the *Crisis*, Husserl (1975, p. 5) articulates the essence of the crisis perhaps as succinctly and accurately as it can be stated: "The positivistic reduction of the idea of science to mere factual science. The 'crisis' of science as the loss of its meaning for life." In his "Vienna Lecture" (included as the First Appendix of the *Crisis*-13), Husserl examines some of the ways in which although faith in science as the finished form of enlightenment rationality may have seemed natural and even positive in the prior decades of the 18th and 19th centuries, current circumstances had clearly shown such faith to be untenable:

> we are being led again into the fateful error of believing that science makes man wise, that it is destined to create a genuine and contented humanity that is master of its fate. . . . Who would take such a notion seriously today?
>
> (Husserl, 1975, pp. 12–13)

This was the question posed circa 1935. The legacy of the science of the Enlightenment had been for Europe an age of invention, technological advances, industrialization, wealth, progress, and learning both in the sciences and in the arts and humanities. This flowering of civilization was, however, followed almost immediately in the 20th century by the horrific, dispiriting, and ultimately largely pointless carnage and disaster of World War I, a worldwide trauma that brought on a global period of economic trouble and political unrest and, in Germany, by 1935, the rise of National Socialism. World War II, only a few years away, served chiefly to amplify the crisis and reveal the depth of its roots in the culture.

Husserl concluded his "Vienna Lecture" with a tragically prophetic statement about the immediate consequences of the crisis. The passage speaks to our own time and possibilities:

> The reason for the failure of a rational culture, however, as we said, lies not in the essence of rationalism itself but solely in its being rendered superficial in its entanglement in 'naturalism' and 'objectivism'. There are only two escapes from the crisis of European existence: the downfall of Europe in its estrangement from its own rational sense of life, its fall into hostility toward the sprit and into barbarity; or the rebirth of Europe from the spirit of philosophy through a heroism of reason that overcomes naturalism once and for all . . . out of the destructive blaze of lack of faith, the smoldering fire of despair over the West's mission for humanity . . . will rise up the phoenix of a new life-inwardness and spiritualization as a pledge of a great and distant future for man: for the spirit alone is immortal.
>
> (Husserl, 1975, p. 299)

It is important to draw from this prescient yet hopeful summary the clear lesson that the crisis that Husserl (and many others) identified was occasioned by the mingling of science (*Wissenschaften*) with naturalism and its attendant claim to explanatory hegemony, as well as its fervent neglect of spirit. Such mingling, Husserl was at pains to show, has broad (and often disastrous) consequences for entire cultures. The manifestation of this same crisis in our own disciplines today is not simply some obscure or minor point about which academics can quibble within lecture halls and conference centers just to keep themselves occupied. It is, rather, of profound importance to humanity because of the magnitude of its consequences. Our culture, our spirit, indeed our future, hang precariously in the balance.

As pointed out earlier, Husserl was by no means the only scholar to identify the crisis of science (*Wissenschaften*). One of the most influential and insightful founders of modern psychology, the Gestalt theorist Wolfgang Köhler, had left Germany to take up residence in the United States in 1935.

After a period of opposition to the rising tide of National Socialism, he left Germany and accepted an academic position at Swarthmore College. His book *The Place of Value in a World of Facts* was published in 1938, the year of Husserl's death, and just 3 years after the Vienna Lecture. In chapter 1 of the book, Köhler makes reference to an article in a German magazine a few years previous, on the topic of the crisis of science (*Wissenschaften*). Köhler acknowledges that his presumption is that this crisis was a topic of general interest and, thus, well known.

The article provides a setting for Köhler's skillful use of an imagined (or at least creatively enhanced) dialogue on the topic with an acquaintance who was also the editor of a magazine. The editor assumes the role of the educated nonscholar who sees the substance and effects of the crisis. Köhler places himself in the role of a scientist—a psychologist—who naturally seeks to defend science. One wonders at Köhler's actual commitment to the position he defends, however, as some of the most cogent and persuasive arguments and sharpest points are made not by Köhler but rather by his conversational antagonist. It is clear from the final chapters of his book that Köhler has hope for the possibilities of a genuinely scientific psychology—one formulated along the lines of his own Gestalt thinking. Köhler firmly believes that such a psychology can do its legitimate scientific job while nonetheless avoiding the problems contributing to the general crisis in the Western intellectual tradition. It is equally obvious that he clearly sees what those problems are and what the dangerous implications inherent in them are, especially through the voice of his editor friend.

Köhler, via the voice he grants his friend, summarizes nicely the issue at the heart of the crisis by noting the considerable "progress" that has resulted from science and technology, and the effect it has on one's "feeling inclined to celebrate the irresistible force of the scientific mind" (Köhler, 1938, p. 8). A careful reader cannot miss the irony embedded in this sentence. Köhler's interlocutor goes on to say that he too thinks "quite as highly of the services which research has rendered to hygiene and to medicine" and that "science has rendered a great service for humanity" (p. 8). However, he continues (and here is the key to the crisis): "Agreeable though this special form of progress may be in several aspects, it also deflects the attention of those who enjoy it from much more essential issues of man" (p. 8). We should note here the double meaning of "those who enjoy it [the progress of science]." This must sure include not only the lay public who benefit, but the scientists themselves who enjoy not only those same products, but the intellectual satisfaction as well as the impressive social status that the success of science bestows on them.

Later in the dialogue, the magazine editor gets to the heart of the problem and adds a new dimension to the crisis. It is that not only has science shown itself largely uninterested and unable to contribute positively to the resolution of the real issues of our humanity, but that science in the past few centuries has actively destroyed other meanings and 'convictions' that people had previously clung to:

> Why are the people in such bitter need of a new orientation in our days? There have been periods of quite as much distress in earlier times. But in those periods the population of Europe had general convictions which gave it strength to stand the strain patiently. There are no such convictions now. Why? Because of the tremendous destructive power with which during the last few hundred years learning and research have fought any stable mental orientation that existed before the era of science.
>
> (Köhler, 1938, p. 11)

The clear implication here is that rather than science (as the legacy and embodiment of the Enlightenment) being the solution to the problems of humanity, or the path leading to answers to our most pressing and perennial questions, it is in fact a central source of the humanity's existential and moral predicament.[2]

As the literature of the Crisis in European thought (*Wissenschaften*) shows, the Crisis came about because too much is expected of Enlightenment thought and its various manifestations, including natural science. History suggests that Enlightenment thought as manifest in science, art, politics, and moral theory, each considered individually, could have neither produced nor prevented the social and moral tragedies of the 19th and 20th centuries. Stepping back one level of analysis—framed by the concerns of Husserl's *Crisis*—the science of the Enlightenment could not subsume or respond effectively to the crucial issues and questions of our humanity, as lived in specific cultures or in individual lives. Focused more tightly, we can state the same thing by concluding that the science (*Wissenschaften*) of the day, despite its respectable Enlightenment pedigree, could not adequately understand or control the distinctly human world. It could not provide adequate understanding of humanity itself. Ultimately, no more can be expected of any 'science', or way of knowing, than the particulars of that approach and its subject matter are capable, by their very nature, of providing.

The problems of the Crisis, the "malaise of modernity" (Taylor, 1991), and now scientism come when more is expected of an intellectual endeavor—in this case science—than it is equipped to provide because it is neither sensitive to, nor formulated around a core of understandings of, the essential nature of the phenomenon it is supposed to explain and reveal—in this case, our humanity. This unrealistic expectation about the powers of natural science, promoted and promulgated among believers with considerable passion, is the essential problematic core of the modern intellectual phenomenon of *scientism*. The fundamental problem at the heart of the historical *Crisis* is not that the Enlightenment *Wissenschaften* was fundamentally wrong or lacking, or that it was not pursued with sufficient rigor and determination as the solution to the problems facing 19th and 20th century Western cultures. The problem was that it (Enlightenment science) was expected to provide something that it was simply capable of providing: the revelation to ourselves of our own humanity, and, therefore, the solution to our human situation and its attendant defining issues, that is, meaning, morality, and purpose.

This mistake is being repeated from the latter 20th and into the 21st century as part of the core "malaise of modernity" (Taylor, 1991). The term *scientism* has come into use by critical scholars to describe this enterprise. Scientism demands of a particular circumscribed species of science what it simply cannot provide, namely apodictic comprehension of our human being, circumscribing in that comprehension the origin, substance, and meaning of humanity itself, and all within a restrictive language of naturalistic materialism. The principle purpose of this introductory chapter is to lay out the basic project of scientism as a context for the more particular examinations of that project within contemporary psychology and related social sciences to be found in the chapters of this volume. One of the very important things to understand about scientism is the distinction between scientism and science itself. The reason appreciating the distinction between science and scientism is important is not only because the two are often confounded by those newly involved in the topic, but also because advocates of scientism often make the explicit claim that scientism just *is* science. Indeed, this fact provided the reason for the title of this book. To give science over to scientism (i.e., to hijack science) is not only intellectually naïve, but dangerous both culturally and morally.

What Is Science?

The truth is that 'science' is not as easy to define as it might first seem. It turns out to be one of those things about which we are tempted to say, "I cannot define it, but I know it when I see it." The etymology of the word 'science' simply informs us that the word's original meaning was simply 'knowledge'. As there are various kinds of knowledge produced in various ways, knowing this simply does not illuminate much. One might restrict scientific knowledge to that knowledge gained only through the scientific method. However, surprising as it might be to some, there seems to be no such thing as *the* scientific method. Accounts of the history of science inform us that the methods of science developed gradually and with variations necessitated by particular subjects and methods of study (see, for example, the short but very informative history by Principe, 2011). Both science and scientific methods seem to have grown organically as bright minds applied themselves to important questions. The methods of science were not discovered; rather, they were created, developed, and adapted in response to very pragmatic concerns. It seems rather impossible to specify a single 'scientific method' that has been or is used by all scientists at all times or in all places. There does not seem to be a single method used in the work of geneticists, botanical taxonomists, volcanologists, neuroscientists, astronomers, quantum physicists, or social demographers. In the discipline of psychology, 'science' is almost always defined in terms of the empirical experiment—often of a sort not common to other sciences.

It is a bit easier to talk about what science is if we focus on what might be called the 'empirical approach'. Bas van Fraassen (2004, 2015) has provided a helpful history of the relationship between empiricism, naturalism, and science. A good working definition of 'science' is one that emphasizes that science is knowledge produced by observing and reporting the phenomena of the empirical world. In other words, science is a way of knowing that sticks to observation and the careful and faithful reporting of observable things in the world. The definition of 'science' really does not need to be more elaborate than this. Problems, however, often result when we attempt to make it more elaborate.

Science *qua* science needs to make very few assumptions about the nature of the world. To make meaningful observations and sensible reports it must be assumed that (a) the world is orderly and (b) that the rational mind can recognize and understand that orderliness. Notice here that science does not require that any particular metaphysic be operative in the observable world. That is, science can proceed regardless of the source or cause of the order underlying the phenomena that are the objects of scientific observation. Of course, scientists do try to formulate plausible explanations of the phenomena they observe and report, and they are often able to give detailed accounts of how certain phenomena come about. This endeavor takes scientists back somewhat to their roots in the natural philosophy of the 16th through the 19th centuries. However, it is crucial to note that science can proceed and do its job regardless of the ultimate nature and origin of the phenomena under study. For example, biological science can proceed much as it has, and produce knowledge much as it does, whether the ultimate account of the source of the order of the phenomena of the biological world comes from some process of natural selection as neo-Darwinism purports, or whether the fingerprints of an intelligent God are ultimately found all over the biological world. Science as understood and practiced for centuries is metaphysically innocent. In other words, science *qua* science does not require that any particular metaphysic actually be in place in the natural or in the human world. At the same time, science is also epistemologically innocent. While science employs empiricism as a method, confining its activities to what occurs in the observable world, science does not require that sensory experience be the only source of human knowledge or understanding. In these two points we find the chief distinction between science and scientism.

What Is Scientism?

In the literature and commentary on scientism, it is usually described in terms of three or four intellectual commitments regarding the nature of science (see, e.g., Williams & Robinson, 2015). It should be pointed out, however, that the term 'scientism' is not the name of any school of thought or philosophical perspective. In fact, it is not a term that even those whose perspectives are clearly scientistic would generally apply to themselves. Usually, the term 'scientism' is employed as a criticism of an intellectual or philosophical position. Interestingly, in recent years some intellectuals have embraced the term 'scientism' as a positive label for their intellectual positions (see, e.g., Pinker, 2013). As an '-ism', scientism denotes an extreme position, one in which the implication is that one has gone beyond mere 'science' to something else, something ideological. This characterization of scientism seems apt. Scientism indeed seeks to go beyond science as traditionally developed, practiced, and understood, and does so because of ideological commitment rather than scientific necessity. It is thus an attempt to hijack science in the service of metaphysical and ideological commitments that are not intrinsic to science itself.

Exaggerated Confidence in Empirical Science

One defining characteristic of scientism is manifest in an exaggerated and, therefore, extreme confidence in 'science' to produce the requisite knowledge for solving all problems and answering all meaningful questions. This feature of scientism is as common in contemporary psychology as it has been in the natural sciences of the previous two centuries. In psychology, in practical terms, what this amounts to is an extreme confidence in empirical experimental research to provide data that will yield knowledge that permits the control and prediction of human behavior—ostensibly so that problematic behaviors can be eliminated and more appropriate ones established. This expectation seems at odds with a common recognition that has been noted by scholars for decades—that is, experimental psychology simply cannot adequately address certain key aspects of human life and behavior. Specifically omitted from the domain of experimental psychological investigation is a variety of moral, spiritual, and other meaningful phenomena. However, it is precisely these phenomena that are at the heart of much, if not most, of what psychology would seek to address in the interest of helping the world by scientific means. To assume that such things can be addressed at the cold, rational-scientific level (notwithstanding the processes of operationalization) simply recapitulates the problem manifest in the *Crisis* of the *Wissenschaften* identified by Husserl, as well as the "malaise of modernity" (Taylor, 1991) that pervades our contemporary culture. In this sense, psychology seems as irrelevant in our day as the *Wissenschaften* did in the interwar period in Europe.

The Unity of Science

This manifestation of scientism has roots in the thought of the Vienna Circle and the logical positivism of the late 19th and early 20th centuries. Scientism claims that all sciences are, when properly understood and crafted, essentially the same. That is, they share the same methods and assumptions, including their grounding metaphysical and epistemological commitments, and are, thus, consilient. It is, therefore, further affirmed that the most successful of the sciences (i.e., the natural sciences) provide the best model for all scientific practice in all disciplines and subject areas. It follows also that the methods and the assumptions of the natural sciences are appropriate—even required—for any field of scholarly investigation to be a science at all.

Only Certifiably Scientific Knowledge Counts as Knowledge at All

If one believes firmly in the first two tenets of scientism as described earlier, then it is a small step, and for many a compelling one, to the proposition that only science is capable of producing real knowledge. The content and product of all other human endeavors, including religion, art, and the humanities, are grounded only in opinion or subjective impression. Advocates of scientism are confident that scientifically produced knowledge will eventually repudiate or replace all other forms of expression or understanding currently touted as knowledge. This tenet of scientism challenges the legitimacy and relevance of much of our Western intellectual and cultural tradition—specifically the part closest to the most meaningful aspects of our humanity. In so doing, scientism also imposes a very strict epistemological regime on our intellectual lives and our culture.

Naturalistic Materialism Offers a Full Account of the Nature of the World

As noted earlier, science involves careful observation and reporting of the phenomena of the experiential world. As such, it requires only that the world of experience be orderly and intelligible. It does not require any particular metaphysical system be the source of the order and rationality and thus is metaphysically innocent. Scientism, however, as a doctrine about science—rather than as science itself—is the instantiation of a metaphysical commitment to an exhaustive naturalistic materialism. In simple terms, scientism demands the world be as the methods of the natural sciences developed in the 19th and 20th centuries have assumed it must be. There is, however, no legitimate scientific reason to make such a metaphysical commitment, nor is there a rational justification for making such a commitment in order to do science. The reasons for the commitment seem to be cultural, synthetically rational, or perhaps personal. However, none of these reasons is itself scientific. At best, scientism is a paradigm, in the Kuhnian (Kuhn, 1962) sense, created by a community of scientists, and then deployed as a socially constructed model for how science must be in order to be science. It is, in the final analysis, really just a hijacking of science in the interests of a metaphysical commitment to naturalistic materialism.

Summary

This brief introduction defines the contemporary phenomenon of scientism and locates it within a larger intellectual tradition. Scientism represents a contemporary avatar of what began as the *Crisis* of the sciences in Europe during the interwar period when it became apparent that the sciences, as the capstone of the Enlightenment, had little to offer in terms of understanding human being and the meanings, morality, and purposes that define our humanity. Following World War II, the same crisis came to be described in more contemporary literature as the "malaise of modernism" (Taylor, 1991). Scientism represents a response to the issues of the Crisis and the modern malaise by a hardening of commitment to the same categories of thought and understanding that were previously inadequate and irrelevant to understanding the truly human. The hope of scientism seems to be to demonstrate the utility of science in answering all questions of our humanity by insisting on the reality of a metaphysic that (by fiat) brings human problems into the realm of science and by hijacking science in the service of validating that metaphysical doctrine. However, no substantive question related to what it means to be a human being is ever satisfied by defining it out of existence. Contemporary psychology, however, has been drawn into scientism as the "new orthodoxy"

(Williams & Robinson, 2015). The chapters in this volume seek to illuminate the nature of scientism and its effects on the discipline of psychology, and on our understanding of the subject matter of the discipline: human being itself.

Notes

1 For clarity, it should be noted here that, although the German term *Wissenschaften*, although frequently translated as 'science', is really much broader than what the word 'science' conjures up in the contemporary modern mind—including the disciplinary 'mind' of contemporary psychology. The 'science' referred to as *Wissenschaften* in this 'crisis literature' should be understood to include virtually all intellectual work in the tradition that is taken to be the fulfillment and culmination of the Enlightenment. The crown jewel of the Enlightenment is science, particularly as manifest in its finished and most refined form in the natural sciences.

2 Nothing in the foregoing analysis of the enlightenment as it has unfolded in Western thought, and the failure of Western culture to avoid the political and cultural tragedies of the 20th century or the even more recent "malaise of modernity" (Taylor, 1991), is intended as a criticism or rejection of enlightenment thought, per se. Generic rejection of 'The Enlightenment' has come into vogue in recent decades as part of a properly enlightened postmodern consciousness. However, serious, educated persons can hardly dismiss in a single stroke or inveigh against the results of enlightenment thought and the advances it has made possible in science, technology, and medicine (see Stark, 2014). Enlightenment thinking likewise made crucial contributions to legal and political thought, systems of government, and moral philosophy. We have no interest in contributing to any generic dismissive anti-enlightenment or anti-science discourse.

References

Brown, P. (2017). The sons destined to murder their fathers: Crisis in Interwar Germany. In M. Sharpe, R. Jeffs, & J. Reynolds (Eds.), *100 years of European philosophy since the Great War: Crisis and reconfigurations* (pp. 67–82). Dordrecht: Springer.

Gay, P. (1977a). *The enlightenment: The rise of modern paganism.* New York: W. W. Norton.

Gay, P. (1977b). *The enlightenment: The science of freedom.* New York: W. W. Norton.

Herman, A. (2013). *The cave and the light: Plato versus Aristotle, and the struggle for the soul of Western civilization.* New York: Random House.

Husserl, E. (1975). *The crisis of the European sciences and transcendental phenomenology: An introduction to phenomenological philosophy* (D. Carr, Trans.). Evanston, IL: Northwestern University Press. (Original work published 1936)

Jeffs, R., & Sharpe, M. (2017). Introduction: European thought, after the Deluge. In M. Sharpe, R. Jeffs, & J. Reynolds, J. (Eds.), *100 years of European philosophy since the Great War: Crisis and reconfigurations* (pp. 1–26). Dordrecht: Springer.

Köhler, W. (1938). *The place of value in a world of facts.* New York: Meridian Books.

Kuhn, T. S. (1962). *The structure of scientific revolutions*. Chicago, IL: University of Chicago Press.

Pinker, S. (2013, August 6). Science is not your enemy: An impassioned plea to neglected novelists, embattled professors, and tenure-less historians. *New Republic*.

Principe, L. M. (2011). *The scientific revolution: A very short introduction*. Oxford: Oxford University Press.

Sharpe, M., Jeffs, R., & Reynolds, J. (Eds.). (2017). *100 years of European philosophy since the Great War: Crisis and reconfigurations*. Dordrecht: Springer.

Stark, R. (2014). *How the west won: The neglected story of the triumph of modernity*. Wilmington, DE: ISI Books.

Taylor, C. (1991). *The malaise of modernity*. Scarborough, ON: HarperCollins.

Van Fraassen, B. C. (2004). *The empirical stance*. Princeton, NJ: Yale University Press.

Van Fraassen, B. C. (2015). Naturalism in epistemology. In R. N. Williams & D. N. Robinson (Eds.), *Scientism: The new orthodoxy* (pp. 63–96). London: Bloomsbury.

Williams, R. N., & Robinson, D. N. (Eds.). (2015). *Scientism: The new orthodoxy*. London: Bloomsbury.

1 Epistemology and the Boundaries Between Phenomena and Conventions

Daniel N. Robinson

It is in some quarters a veritable truism that, of the various modes of inquiry and explanation, it is science that stands as the gold standard, its record of success unequalled by such historical alternatives as authority, revelation, ordinary perception, popular agreement, or even episodic success at the practical level. The strong version of this perspective grounds a species of *scientific realism* expressed, as summarized by Psillos (2006), in a small but trenchant set of propositions. There is first a *Metaphysical Thesis* that takes the structure of reality to be mind-independent. To this is added the *Semantic Thesis* identifying authentic scientific theories as truth-conditional. They are, as it were, falsifiable at the level of fact. There is also an *Epistemic Thesis* requiring predictive success. There are no miracles in accounts of this success. Rather, explanation moves by way of inferential chains constructed out of facts and having as the ultimate goal that *best explanation*, easier to label than to find. A few words are required in considering the properties that render explanations defective, good, better, and best.

The first obstacle to reaching a defensible position on the rank ordering of explanations is the prior requirement of a defensible position on what there is to explain. That vexing term, *metaphysics*, began innocently enough. Early translators and commentators on Aristotle noted that Aristotle took up the question of 'being' itself in a work that refers to a recently completed inquiry into natural science. The Greek for that inquiry is conveyed by the word φυσις. Thus, the enlarged and later treatise was rendered simply as 'after the physics treatise'—μετα τα φυσικα.

Although the title began as something of a filing technique, it was readily recognized as a deep, critical inquiry into the nature of knowledge, the things that are knowable, and the standards of understanding as one seeks to unearth the causes of things. Clear in this formidable inquiry is the interdependence of epistemology and ontology—the interdependence of various modes of knowing and prior commitments as to what there is to know.

Here is a work that begins with a nearly childlike empiricism:

> ALL men by nature desire to know. An indication of this is the delight we take in our senses; for even apart from their usefulness they are loved for themselves; and above all others the sense of sight. For not only with a view to action, but even when we are not going to do anything, we prefer seeing (one might say) to everything else. The reason is that this, most of all the senses, makes us know and brings to light many differences between things.[1]

This is just the beginning. It is followed by a distinction between detailed factual knowledge and that form of *wisdom* that reaches universals otherwise not accessible at the level of observation. Book II even supports something of a social constructionist position on truth:

> No one is able to attain the truth adequately, while, on the other hand, we do not collectively fail, but everyone says something true about the nature of things, and while individually we contribute little or nothing to the truth, by the union of all a considerable amount is amassed.

It is in Part II of Book IV that Aristotle provides an outline of the task undertaken by what later would be called the metaphysician. He says:

> Since there are many senses in which a thing is said to be one, these terms also will have many senses . . . It is evident, then, that it belongs to one science to be able to give an account of these concepts as well as of substance . . . and that it is the function of the philosopher to be able to investigate all things. For if it is not the function of the philosopher, who is it who will inquire whether Socrates and Socrates seated are the same thing . . .?

When one leaves the domain of philosophy to inquire into the world of shifting facts, one forgets that the underlying substance in virtue of which there can be such facts is prior to the facts themselves.

Clearly, at least on this account, scientific realism's *Epistemic Thesis* arrives on an ineliminable *metaphysical* foundation that has already legislated on questions of real being, substance, and admissible phenomena. To know the factual structure of reality is to know reality and, even if some sort of cognitive prowess is needed for the task, the reality itself is not the gift of the knower. Indeed, the act of knowing is finally to be explained in terms of those facts that constitute the structure of perception and cognition. Somewhere on the road to that chain of inferences to the best explanation there is the sturdy link of *physicalism* as the authoritative science of mental life. The pages supporting and defying this gambit or prospect now fill a small college library.

One imagines a game show in which our current masters of thought compete for a prize reserved for anyone who can say anything on the physicalism-dualism tension not said 100 times in this month's catalog of journals in philosophy and cognitive science. It is not clear, by the way, why the primary opposition must be confined to versions of *dualism*. What science or philosophical analysis leads to the conclusion that a complete inventory of what really exists includes no more than two kinds of stuff. Why not *trialism* or even *octalism*? This is no time for caviling, so dualism will have to do. How might it contend with whole textbooks in clinical neurology, not to mention a score of peer-review journals routinely casting anti-physicalists as papal legates?

Perhaps one might summon Mary, just one more time, as the defense avails itself of *the Mary problem*. She is a creation of Frank Jackson's who, in the fickle manner of a cad, left poor Mary to be challenged incessantly by teams of prosecutors. While still faithful to her, Jackson introduced her this way:

> Mary is a brilliant scientist who is, for whatever reason, forced to investigate the world from a black and white room via a black and white television monitor. She specializes in the neurophysiology of vision and acquires, let us suppose, all the physical information there is to obtain about what goes on when we see ripe tomatoes, or the sky, and use terms like 'red', 'blue', and so on. She discovers, for example, just which wavelength combinations from the sky stimulate the retina, and exactly how this produces via the central nervous system the contraction of the vocal chords and expulsion of air from the lungs that results in the uttering of the sentence 'The sky is blue' . . . What will happen when Mary is released from her black and white room or is given a color television monitor? Will she learn anything or not? It seems just obvious that she will learn something about the world and our visual experience of it. But then it is inescapable that her previous knowledge was incomplete. But she had all the physical information. Ergo there is more to have than that, and Physicalism is false.
>
> (Jackson, 1982, pp. 127–136)

Many very clever rebuttals were offered against Jackson's initial conclusion. Lycan argues that Mary's use of "blue" is a term drawn from introspection and "would certainly not be synonymous with any primitive or composite expression of public English" (Lycan, 1996, p. 101). David Papineau (1996) contends that, although Mary now has "blue" among items accessible by imagination, the new experience of color has affected her at the level of belief, not new knowledge (pp. 259–271). Still other commentators accept that Mary has gained knowledge, but it is a *phenomenal* knowledge of facts already known (see, e.g., Pereboom, 1994, pp. 315–329). Jackson would come to retract his claim and, with penitential sobriety, embrace physicalism.

He has come to view Mary's achievement not as epistemic but representational, and that the process of representation is well within the explanatory resources of physicalism (Jackson, 2007, pp. 52–64). His reasons, and those whose defenses of physicalism he shares, are not telling and may not even reach the facts that physicalism must explain. Mary has new knowledge, not new 'representations' or 'phenomenal concepts'. Indeed, there is an unintended irony in defenses of physicalism that prove to be transparently *Cartesian* in their reliance on the mental! When Mary sees an object as blue, she does so *because it is blue*, not because it falls under a phenomenal concept (although it might), or because that is just the way she 'represents' stimuli falling in the short-wavelength end of the visible spectrum.

"Blue" has no reference except as a phenomenon presupposing an experient. In the world of the color-blind, there are electromagnetic radiations consisting of different wavelengths, but not consisting of different colors. Color perception is thus basic to any scientific account of color vision, although irrelevant to a physicalistic account of electromagnetic radiation. The same can be said of the taste of one's first onion or the sound when first hearing music. It is a brute fact that an exhaustive knowledge of the laws of harmony cannot generate a sound, nor can a complete description of the classical pain pathways result in pain. One with sufficient philosophical agility can devise any number of accounts that would seem to spare the physicalistic account of conscious experience, but the gap refuses to close. Mary knows what blue looks like, and that's the end of it.

How, then, to spare epistemology from the tar brush of subjectivity? Psychology has long been hostage to a handful of words, perhaps the most demanding of them being 'scientific'. It has parted with its very subject matter as ransom paid under the threat of exposure as an imposter. Psychology is not some nearly feral creature staring about in a gross rusticity as it enters a laboratory. Fechner's psychophysics would reach a maturity in the 20th century in which its functional laws were more precise and reliable than electrophysiological measures of the same processes. One should note, by the way, that these achievements often required no more than two or three subjects and very little guidance from arid treatises on analysis of variance. But the psychology so adept at unearthing fundamental laws of vision and audition may have little to contribute to an understanding of seeing and hearing, and even less to say about the aesthetic dimension of life.

The task yet to be undertaken in a systematic way requires that the discipline form no entangling methodological alliances until it has settled on the subjects calling for explanation. These subjects are not difficult to find. They are the staples of a folk psychology the neglect of which is a pointless sacrifice.

Note

1 The *Metaphysics* is available online at http://classics.mit.edu/Aristotle/metaphysics.1.i.html

References

Jackson, F. (1982). Epiphenomenal qualia. *Philosophical Quarterly*, *32*, 127–136.

Jackson, F. (2007). The knowledge argument, diaphanousness, representationalism. In T. Alter & S. Walter (Eds.), *Phenomenal concepts and phenomenal knowledge: New essays on consciousness and physicalism* (pp. 52–64). Oxford: Oxford University Press.

Lycan, W. G. (Ed.). (1996). *Mind and cognition*. Oxford: Basil Blackwell.

Papineau, D. (1996). The antipathetic fallacy. In T. Metzinger (Ed.), *Conscious experience* (pp. 259–271). Oxford: Oxford University Press.

Pereboom, D. (1994). Bats, scientists, and the limitations of introspection. *Philosophy and Phenomenological Research*, *54*(2), 315–329.

Psillos, S. (2006). Thinking about the ultimate argument for realism. In C. Cheyne & J. Worrall (Eds.), *Rationality & reality: Essays in Honour of Alan Musgrave* (pp. 133–156). Dordrecht: Springer.

2 Hayek and Hempel on the Nature, Role, and Limitations of Science

Richard N. Williams

This chapter examines two influential papers, relevant to the issue of scientism in contemporary psychology. The first is the 1948 article in *Philosophy of Science* by Carl Gustav Hempel and Paul Oppenheim, titled "Studies in the Logic of Explanation" (Hempel & Oppenheim, 1948). The second paper, by the Nobel Prize–winning economist Friedrich Hayek, was published in the journal *Economica* in three parts, one each year, between 1942 and 1944. The title was "Scientism and the Study of Society" (Hayek, 1942, 1943, 1944). Space limitations will permit only a summary of some of the key arguments made in these two articles. However, these articles, published so close together and at a key juncture in the development of contemporary psychology, shed important light on a crucial issue: the nature, origin, and effect of scientism in the discipline. The piece by Hempel and Oppenheim has traditionally been taken to be the authoritative exposition of how psychology can be a genuinely positivist science. It is that exposition that points the discipline in the direction of scientism. Hayek is one of the first and most important scholars to identify and alert the social sciences about the problems incumbent in the turn to scientism.

Studies in the Logic of Explanation: Hempel and Oppenheim

Hempel and Oppenheim (1948) are explicit about the aims of their analysis: they seek to articulate "the basic pattern of scientific explanation [and a] . . . rigorous analysis of the concept of law and of the logical structure of explanatory arguments" (p. 135). It is clear from the arguments they make that they are committed to a unified understanding of science—in the tradition of logical positivism. Hempel and Oppenheim make it clear in their opening paragraph that science is *the* advanced form of rational inquiry:

> To explain the phenomena in the world of our experience, to answer the question of 'why?' rather than only the question 'what?', is one of

the foremost objectives of all rational inquiry; and especially, scientific research in its various branches strives to go beyond a mere description of its subject matter by providing an explanation of the phenomena it investigates.

(p. 135)

Here Hempel and Oppenheim give voice to a basic dimension of scientistic thinking; that is, the role of theory is not understanding human phenomena *per se*, but rather explaining them in some causal terms exterior to them. Hempel and Oppenheim go on to specify "the basic pattern of scientific explanation," maintaining that explanations consist of relationships between sentences "describing the phenomenon to be explained," and "sentences which are adduced to account for the phenomenon" (see pp. 136–138). Only two types of sentences qualify as acceptable scientific explanations: (1) "sentences . . . which state specific antecedent conditions" and (2) "sentences . . . which represent general laws" (p. 137).

Hempel and Oppenheim lay out (a) the logical and (b) the empirical conditions that must be satisfied for any scientific explanation to be considered 'adequate':

1. The phenomenon to be explained must be a "logical consequence" "deducible from the information contained in the" explanation.
2. The explanation "must contain general laws from which the phenomenon derives."
3. The explanation "must have empirical content; i.e., it must be capable, at least in principle, of test by experiment or observation."

The empirical condition for adequacy of an explanation is that:

4. "The sentences constituting the [explanation] must be true." Truth is defined as "factual correctness," and this in turn is defined in terms of its being "highly confirmed by all the relevant evidence available."

Because subsequent evidence may refute the adequacy of any prior explanation, it is advisable in this model of science to speak of truth in probabilistic terms.

Next, Hempel and Oppenheim turn attention to "explanation in the nonphysical sciences" (p. 140). It is clear that the authors fully support the idea that human sciences such as psychology can and should be brought under the umbrella of positivist science. Three important complicating factors specifically addressed are *motivation, teleology,* and *emergence.* The authors' argument is that scientific explanation in biology, psychology, and other social sciences has the same formal structure as scientific explanation in physics.

1. In response to the argument that events in the human world are unique and their originary causes unknown, Hempel and Oppenheim respond that (a) the same can be said about many phenomena in the physical world, and (b) science proceeds anyway by searching out regularities in the relationships between any number of specifiable antecedent conditions and the phenomenon in question. Thus, science can establish the case for lawful regularity by empirical demonstration.

2. In response to the argument that the 'past history' of human beings might interfere with establishing causal relationships operating in the present, the authors point to physical phenomena that can be affected by past states of affairs and suggest this is no real barrier to scientific study and explanation of behavior.

3. In response to suggestions that human beings, unlike physical entities, must be explained by motivational and other teleological factors that appear to function more like 'pulls' from the future than 'pushes' from the past or present, Hempel and Oppenheim state that a properly scientific explanation finds the causal power of motivations and goals in their corresponding physical manifestation in the present state of the person as organism. Thus, the causal force is not from any future condition, nor is it uniquely mental or psychological.

The concept of 'emergence' in human behavior refers to the fact that behaviors, and even motivational states of human beings, are often unpredictable. They seem to 'emerge' from within the person himself or herself, for example, as an act of will, rather than arising as determined by specifiable factors or constituent parts of the person or his or her environment. After a rather lengthy and technical analysis, Hempel and Oppenheim conclude that the more rational approach to what appear to be cases of emergence is to conclude that such phenomena cannot be shown to be the mere effects of a set of known causes—physical or chemical—*at present*. But they suggest the phenomena will ultimately be shown to be thus caused when the science sufficiently advances. This is better because the reality of emergence "involves and perpetuates certain logical misunderstandings, . . . [and] not unlike the ideas of neo-vitalism, it encourages an attitude of resignation which is stifling for scientific research" (p. 52).

In summary, then, Hempel and Oppenheim provided one of the more direct articulations of scientism that have been influential in the history of the discipline of psychology.

Scientism and the Study of Society: F.A. Hayek

Friedrich Hayek had been active in intellectual circles in Vienna during the interwar years and would have been well acquainted with the work of the Vienna Circle. A second cousin to Ludwig Wittgenstein, he acknowledged that his own thought had been influenced by that of Wittgenstein. The concerns and arguments in the three papers published in *Economica* (1942, 1943, 1944) later became part of a book, *The Counter-Revolution of Science*, first published in the United States in 1952, just 4 years after the publication of the Hempel and Oppenheim article.

Immersed—uncritically—in a particular model of psychology as a science, contemporary psychological scholars are likely to mistakenly hear any critical discussion of scientism either as a critique of science itself or as a very narrow critique of the adequacy and efficacy of scientific methods in the study of human behavior. However, Hayek's criticism is much broader. Hayek's broader approach includes considerable time spent on scientism in the two social sciences closest to his own training, history, and economics. The extent of the social and intellectual effects of scientism in these disciplines is an important part of what psychologists need to understand in order to see what is at stake in their own discipline, and to see how psychology might be complicit in the problems and consequences identified by Hayek. What follows represents a brief outline of Hayek's arguments. Some of the conclusions drawn are my own. There follows what I think would be Hayek's response to what many psychologists might ask: Why does all of this this matter anyway? What is at stake?

The Tyranny of Method

Hayek (1942) suggests that the success of the physical and biological sciences contributed to a methodological 'tyranny' exercised upon the social sciences—as willing victims—which after more than a century has "contributed scarcely anything to our understanding of social phenomena" (p. 267). This conclusion echoes the 'Crisis of the Wissenschaften', or the 'crisis of European Sciences' during the interwar period in Europe, a problem with which Hayek was very familiar. It was a widespread concern that science was not contributing to the understanding or solution to the real human concerns of society at that time.

The Impossibility of Genuine Reduction

Science (in its scientist form) has concentrated on a systematic substitution of purely mathematical language for other native languages within which people understand their world. The expectation has been that ordinary language can ultimately be eliminated.

However, Hayek argues persuasively that the reductive project is self-contradictory because the scientistic project seeks to reduce and eliminate as unnecessary the very language and meanings it simultaneously needs in order to evaluate the accuracy of the substitution of language reduction in the number of phenomena to be accounted for.

Objective Versus Subjective Science

Although the terms 'objectivity' and 'subjectivity' are problematic in a number of ways, Hayek argues that the social sciences are 'subjective' in at least three important ways. First, the object of their study has a subjective mind and a life lived in a world that is always already interpretive. Second, therefore, the subject matter of the social sciences (i.e., social and behavioral phenomena) are subjective in their essential nature. Third, scientists have subjective mental lives and are already grounded in *their own subjectivity*. The fact is that our humanity (i.e., our subjectivity or mental life) is at every moment already present and given. Thus there simply is no place to start a scientific study of genuine human phenomena that does not include subjective givenness. To insist otherwise is simply scientistic hubris.

The Nature of Laws and the Laws of Nature

Hayek (1942) summarizes the difference in what law must be and what 'law' must surely mean in the two sciences (natural and human): "What is relevant in the study of society is not whether these laws of nature are true in any objective sense, but solely whether they are believed and acted upon by the people" (p. 280). The point is that whatever 'laws' might be, they are understood and function very differently in the natural and the human worlds. Scientism overlooks this fact and, thus, ignores meaning by seeking to derive it from meaningless physical (or metaphysical) stuff.

Objective and Subjective Mind

Hayek affirms the observation, often attributed to Wittgenstein, that every human being has privileged access to his or her own mental experience (see also the argument by Swinburne, 2015). Thus, no external observer can be confident at all of the contents of another (subjective) conscious mind. It follows from this that no external (objective) causes can be invoked by an observer for any conscious phenomenon belonging to another person, since the nature of that conscious phenomenon cannot be specified or verified by any other (objective) observer. This position does not end in solipsism, however, because communal trial and error, and appreciation of their consequences, allow us to have confidence in our experiences and their regularities. Social entities are not natural categories; they are wholly dependent on (often communal) subjective 'mental schemes' that create them and hold them together. It is the nature of human beings as 'subjective' rational beings that renders scientistic, natural scientific approaches to the social sciences incoherent.

Hayek (1944) makes clear that the problem of scientism is not in the nature of science itself:

> In conclusion it is, perhaps, desirable to remind the reader once more that all we have said here is directed solely against a misuse of Science, not against the scientist in the special field where he is competent, but against the application of his mental habits in fields where he is not competent. There is no conflict between our conclusions and those of legitimate science.
>
> (p. 39)

Consequences of Scientism and Its Super Mind

We now come to the most comprehensive analysis of scientism that Hayek offers, and the cause of greatest concern to serious students of social science and defenders of humanity. Scientism, imbued as it is with 'objective', natural scientific perspectives, views things, including human beings, human activities, social wholes, social entities—all human phenomena—'from the outside'. For this reason, all understanding must come from the outside. Noted psychologist Joseph Rychlak (1977) recognized just this in his distinction between the 'introspective' and 'extraspective' perspectives in psychological theorizing. From a scientistic perspective, prediction requires knowledge of forces and realities that are in play from outside the understanding and control of individual human beings. It is as if there is a causal 'flow' outside us all. For Hayek, all this entails the search for what he refers to as a "super mind." If the source of rationality is not in the individual human minds of individual human beings, then it must be outside. It must reside in a suprahuman rationality manifest in structures, laws, principles, or forces. This super mind affords to the scientistic social scientist what must be understood as a type of privileged perspective from which to view and understand the human world. It is thus the task of (scientistic) science to find those rational, reason-required structures, laws, principles, and forces that lawfully produce human events on the individual and communal levels, to identify them, and then to exercise control over them—and through them, over human affairs.

Hayek gives a good deal of attention to one phenomenon of this super mind: *historicism*. It is historicism—the reification of an invisible rational thrust of history—that has allowed the last century's German National

Socialists, and contemporary Marxists, feminists, and many leaders of social thought, to conclude, sometimes with extreme confidence, that some (who do not agree with them) are 'on the wrong side of history', while others (who agree with them) are enlightened. The confidence endemic to historicism or any other manifestation of knowledge derived from contact with the super mind sometimes engenders calls for reeducation and training so that those who have not seen the actions of the super mind might be trained how to recognize it. Such confidence could only come from someone who has achieved access to the super mind, allowing him or her to predict its course and even control it. The promise of and the desire for *control* is, for Hayek, an almost irresistible attraction of scientism.

This super mind Hayek describes enables social scientists to see the order, rationality, and causes that are opaque, or invisible, to common individuals. It also pretends to offer social scientists powers of prediction available only to those who have access to the super mind, as well as any number of means of and reasons for control over human events, human beings, and human institutions—even suggesting that such control is the only possible rational course for a responsible social science and a responsible society.

In summary, the fundamental problem with scientism is twofold: (1) It offers human beings understandings of themselves as 'stages' rather than 'actors', which understandings can have far-reaching interpersonal, moral, and political consequences; and (2) in the guise of self-appropriated 'super rationality', it legitimates, and even at times recommends, a sort of tyranny.

Here I give Hayek the last word:

> It may well be true that we as scholars tend to overestimate the influence which we can exercise on contemporary affairs. But I doubt whether it is possible to overestimate the influence which ideas have in the long run.
>
> (1952, p. 400)

And:

> we are still, largely without knowing it, under the influence of ideas which have almost imperceptibly crept into modern thought because they were shared by the founders of what seemed to be radically opposed traditions [the positivism of Auguste Comte and the German idealism of G.W.F. Hegel]. In these matters we are to a great extent still guided by ideas which are at least a century old, just as the nineteenth century was mainly guided by the ideas of the eighteenth. But whereas the ideas of Hume and Voltaire, of Adam Smith and Kant, produced the liberalism of the nineteenth century, those of Hegel and

Comte, of Feuerbach and Marx, have produced the totalitarianism of the twentieth.

(1952, p. 399)

And, finally:

The most dangerous stage in the growth of civilization may well be that in which man has come to regard all . . . [non-scientific] beliefs as superstitions and refuses to accept or to submit to anything which he does not rationally understand. The rationalist whose reason is not sufficient to teach him those limitations of the powers of conscious reason and who despises all the institutions and customs which have not been consciously designed would thus become the destroyer of the civilization built upon them. This may well prove a hurdle which man will repeatedly reach only to be thrown back into barbarism.

(1944, p. 33)

Hayek's conclusions about scientism, and it potential effects not only on human beings but also on human institutions and societies, seems dire indeed. However, prudence requires such conclusions from well-argued analyses not be routinely or thoughtlessly dismissed. This is particularly the case when we understand that Hayek is not alone in his analysis of scientism and its real potential of genuine mischief. Sociologist David Martin (1969) described the effects of a scientism taken seriously for a basic understanding of the world and the institutions of contemporary society. One of the effects is as follows:

Debate must give way to technical committee, seminar to laboratory, and the office of administrator can be merged with that of priest, who then becomes a scientific coordinator. . . . Religion and politics are both assimilated to science. . . . [and] just as there is no disagreement in science there can be no disagreement in society: hence, the government of people may give way to the administration of things.

(p. 37)

Michael D. Aeschliman (1998) reached a similar conclusion:

And it is in an important sense the ultimate effect of scientism to dissolve the absolute qualitative distinction between persons and things—the very heart of the metaphysical tradition of *sapientia*—reducing persons *to* things, denying man's rational soul and his transcendence of the physical, giving him a value no higher than that of a camel or a stone or any other part of nature.

(p. 52)

Certainly, no conspiracy theory is being offered here. The intent of this chapter is simply to travel down the intellectual path of scientism as it has been marked out by its leading purveyors to see where it leads. From the point of view of serious, well-qualified, and well-trained thinkers who have looked down the path, there are serious real consequences awaiting us at the destination. This is not surprising because ideas always have consequences. It is not being suggested here that the whole of psychology or that any individual psychologists are nefarious, purposefully seeking power and control and the dissolution of humanity. However, whether one purposefully marches down a path, or innocently and unthinkingly wanders down it, the destination is the same. To be intellectually and professionally oblivious to the consequences of scientism—either at an individual or at a disciplinary level—entails great risks. It is not clear the extent to which the discipline of psychology is intellectually equipped or motivated to either recognize the risks *as* risks or to avoid their consequences.

References

Aeschliman, M. D. (1998). *The restitution of man: C. S. Lewis and the case against scientism*. Grand Rapids, MI: Wm. B. Eerdmans.

Hayek, F. A. (1942). Scientism and the study of society. Part I. *Economica, 9*(35), 267–291.

Hayek, F. A. (1943). Scientism and the study of society. Part II. *Economica, 10*(37), 34–63.

Hayek, F. A. (1944). Scientism and the study of society. Part III. *Economica, 11*(41), 27–39.

Hayek, F. A. (1952). *The counter-revolution of science* (2nd ed.). Glencoe, IL: Free Press.

Hempel, C. G., & Oppenheim, P. (1948). Studies in the logic of explanation. *Philosophy of Science, 15*(2), 137–175.

Martin, D. (1969). *The religious and the secular: Studies in secularization*. New York: Schocken.

Rychlak, J. F. (1977). *The psychology of rigorous humanism*. New York: McGraw-Hill.

Swinburne, R. (2015). The implausibility of physical determinism. In R. N. Williams and D. N. Robinson (Eds.), *Scientism: The new orthodoxy*. London, UK: Bloomsbury Academic.

3 On Scientism in Psychology
Some Observations of Historical Relevance

James T. Lamiell

In consideration of a widespread and long-standing conceptual negligence in psychology, epitomized by its general commitment to the scientism discussed critically throughout this book, Robinson, in the foreword to this volume, brands this book a 'call for clarity' within psychology as it advances—putatively with scientific authority—claims to knowledge about various aspects of nothing less consequential than human nature itself. Of course, the clarity called for here is not of the sort that can be achieved by conducting another experiment or by executing another sophisticated statistical analysis. The problems on which a discipline infected by scientism obstinately turns its collective back are *conceptual* ones, which can only be addressed satisfactorily through close and penetrating conceptual analyses of the sort that scientism proscribes. The only way out of this vicious circularity, it would seem, is by offering discussions such as those contained in this volume to up-and-coming younger scholars who have not already embraced—or who, out of careerist concerns, have meekly but unhappily resigned themselves to—the tenets of scientism. As part of such an effort, the present chapter aims to complement the others by drawing into consideration relevant ideas held by some of our disciplinary forebears, and in this way cast historical light on the roots of the scientistic ethos that so dominates psychology today.

"But It's Merely Theoretical!"

Within the specialty area of personality studies, the subdiscipline of psychology in which I took my graduate training, the single most discussed issue throughout the 1970s and into the 1980s was that of consistency (or the lack thereof) over time and across situations in the behavioral manifestation by individuals of their theoretically stable personality traits. Mischel (1968) had produced evidence that correlations between measures reflecting individual differences in personality traits and behavioral differences that should have been predictable by those trait measures rarely exceeded $r = .30$,[1] and were most often appreciably lower than that. In the eyes of many, Mischel's (1968) findings pointed to the overriding importance of situational factors relative to supposedly stable personality characteristics in the determination of individuals' behaviors. However, other researchers countered with empirical demonstrations that trait–behavior correlations could be high, provided that the research was properly designed and carried out (e.g., Bem & Allen, 1974; Bem & Funder, 1978; Block, 1977; Epstein, 1977, 1979, 1980, 1983). Thus unfolded the so-called person–situation debate.

Following this debate closely, I finally awoke to an utterly fundamental conceptual problem infecting the entire discussion; namely, the unbridgeable logical gap between the theoretical issue in question (i.e., the extent of cross-situational consistency in the behavioral manifestation by individuals of their theoretically stable personality traits on the one side, and the correlation coefficients being accepted by all disputants as the proper way to address this question empirically on the other). From all positions adopted in the debate, it was agreed that 'low' correlations indicated inconsistency while 'high' correlations indicated appreciable consistency.

Repeatedly pressed by students to explain just how it was that the correlation coefficients under discussion indicated what they were said to indicate in this matter, I finally came to see that with respect to the theoretical question of *individual*-level (in)consistency in the manifestation of personality traits, those correlation coefficients were actually *silent*: they were mathematically defined only for populations, not for individuals, and hence could not properly warrant *any* knowledge claims *whatsoever* about *any one* of the individuals investigated.

With regard to the question of temporal or transsituational (in)consistency in the behavioral manifestation of personality traits, the only knowledge claim that could validly have been advanced on the basis of correlation coefficients was that the research participants investigated had not been *equally* (in)consistent.[2] This meant, of course, that some of the participants (although it could not have been said which ones) had been relatively consistent while others had been relatively inconsistent, and this was true irrespective of the magnitude of the correlations.[3]

It is difficult to avoid chuckling while stating that one cannot achieve a proper understanding of this matter by discovering its truth empirically! One arrives at such an understanding through a rational consideration of the manner in which the correlations under examination are mathematically defined. Accordingly, in the wake of the 'Eureka!' moment I experienced by realizing the unbridgeable theory–data gap that had been running through the entire person–situation debate in personality psychology, it seemed clear that a journal article addressing this fundamental conceptual issue was in order. After all, the rational considerations called for in the event had been, up to that time, completely neglected by all participants in the debate, and it seemed that if the debate were ever to bear genuine scientific fruit, its conceptual deficiencies would have to be remedied. More specifically, the debate would have to be recast so that the empirical considerations being brought to bear on the matter conformed logically to the theoretical question at hand. With this in mind, I set about writing the conceptual article I felt was needed. After three versions of the article, submitted over a period of nearly two years, were rejected (deservedly, I eventually came to appreciate), the fourth version was at long last accepted for publication, and the article finally appeared in the March 1981 issue of *American Psychologist* (Lamiell, 1981).

Within a few days of the article's publication, I chanced upon a senior and highly influential member of my departmental faculty in the coffee room. He congratulated me perfunctorily on the accomplishment, and then shot back over his shoulder as he was exiting the room, "But it's merely theoretical!"

"Merely?" I thought. *Merely?* Ought I really to have been busying myself over the previous 2 years with empirical investigations of the sort I was now critiquing when what was needed in my subdiscipline at that particular time was careful *conceptual* analysis? After all, were we not scientists, engaged, as William Whewell (1794–1866) had once put things, not only "in the colligation of facts" but also in "*the clarification of concepts*"?[4]

As an aspiring scholar, I was stunned by my senior colleague's abrupt dismissal of my 2-year devotion to the clarification of a fundamentally important conceptual issue. As a young and untenured assistant professor not yet five full years out of graduate school, I was shaken by the derisive tone of my colleague's "merely," into which I read that if he had anything to say about it (which he did), my long-term prospects in that department were not bright. The validity of my take on this interchange was confirmed 1 year later, when I was informed in a letter signed by my colleague that my research was "not of sufficient quality" to merit promotion and tenure. And so did it happen that before I ever encountered the notion of 'scientism' in scholarly discourse, I had experienced my first harsh and hurtful collision with it.

Viewed within the broad context of a wealth of academic experiences that I have had over the nearly 40 years that have passed since the events just recounted, I can now see those events as part of a discipline-wide devaluation of conceptual/theoretical work that had begun many decades before I came along. Scientism epitomizes this devaluation, and the other contributions to this volume highlight many of the ways in which that devaluation is profoundly problematic (see also Machado & Silva, 2007). Through my own explorations in various works from the late 19th and early 20th centuries, explorations I undertook for reasons tangential to our considerations here, I have encountered cautionary notes about scientism that, had they been more widely and fully heeded at the time, might at least have made scientism's hazards better understood by psychologists then, and, in turn, more avoidable within psychology now.

The first work to be mentioned in this connection is an essay published by the widely acknowledged founder of experimental psychology, Wilhelm Wundt (1832–1920), under the title *Die Psychologie im Kampf ums Dasein* (Wundt, 1913).[5]

Wundt on *Psychology's Struggle for Existence* (1913)

Wundt's objective in his 1913 essay was to counter the rising tide of enthusiasm for a divorce of experimental psychology from philosophy. Although, as he noted, the split was widely favored, albeit for different reasons, in both of the disciplines involved, that is, by the 'pure' philosophers on the one side (those concerned with the traditional subjects of metaphysics, epistemology, ontology, ethics, and the history of philosophy),[6] and by the upstart experimental 'philosophers' (psychologists) on the other, he admonished them all in the essay's foreword as follows:

> If this matter takes the course that both parties want, philosophy will lose more than it will gain, but psychology will be damaged the most. Hence, the argument over the question of whether psychology is or is not a philosophical science is, for psychology, a struggle for its very existence.
>
> (Wundt, 2013, p. 205)[7]

Early in his essay, Wundt sounded the need for clarity by the traditional (or 'pure') philosophers on whether they were seeking to divorce themselves from *all* of psychology or only from *experimental* psychology. He noted in this connection that even he, as the founder of experimental psychology, had seen from the start that some of the discipline's rightful subject matter could not properly be approached experimentally, and would be the proper domain of his own 'other' psychology (cf. Jüttemann, 2006), that is, *Völkerpsychologie* or 'cultural psychology'. Wundt then argued that given that many traditional philosophers, including some of his personal acquaintance, were engaged, both in their research and in their teaching, with subjects proper to the cultural psychology, they must have been intending their support for the divorce of philosophy from psychology to apply only to experimental psychology (see Wundt, 2013, p. 197).

With time, of course, the majority of mainstream psychologists would adopt the view, never accepted by Wundt himself, that the subject matters of such subdisciplines as social psychology, developmental psychology, personality studies, psycholinguistics, and psychological abnormality[8] could likewise be investigated experimentally, or at least quasi-experimentally in acknowledgement of the legitimacy of correlational methods of inquiry (cf. Lamiell, 2013a). The effective consequence of this was that those subdisciplines, too, would eventually be divorced from philosophy no less than the original experimental psychology of which Wundt was writing in 1913. From a strictly intellectual standpoint (which was not the only standpoint Wundt adopted in the 1913 essay; cf. Ash, 1980), Wundt's primary concern over the divorce of psychology from philosophy was that psychologists, preoccupied to an ever-greater extent with technical questions of the sort so important for the design and conduct of laboratory investigations and for the careful analysis of data, would lose sight of, and, with time, the academic wherewithal to grapple with, the abiding *conceptual* matters so vital to the intellectual health of the discipline. The result would be a technically and methodologically sophisticated field of inquiry largely blind to issues the careful and critical consideration of which would be essential to the field's integrity *as a genuine science*. The field would thus degenerate into a merely technical discipline populated not by scientists but by *Handwerker* or 'craftspeople' (see below).

In just this vein, Wundt observed the following about the discussion of the matter as it had developed up to then:

> There is a question that has hardly been touched upon but should be thought about, as it is a decisive one. This is the question of the extent to which it would even be possible for the psychologist to divest himself [*sic*] of philosophy, and to have no need of the assistance of philosophical observations while addressing in depth psychology's own problems. Assuming that such philosophical observations would have value, the question is whether or not psychologists would be able to formulate them on their own.
>
> (Wundt, 2013, p. 208, brackets added)

Wundt's clear answer to this question was "no," and that is why he saw in the looming divorce "the separation of psychology from precisely that domain of science that is indispensable to it" (Wundt, 2013, p. 201). Emphatically underscoring his convictions in this regard, Wundt went on to state:

> [T]he broadest questions, and hence the ones that for an education in psychology are the most important, are so closely connected with epistemological and metaphysical positions that it is inconceivable that they will at some point disappear from psychology. It is precisely this that shows clearly that psychology belongs to the philosophical disciplines, and this will remain so even after the transformation of psychology into

an independent discipline. In a psychology divorced from philosophy, philosophical considerations will be latent, and so it is possible that psychologists who will have abandoned philosophy, and whose education in philosophy will therefore be deficient, will be projecting those considerations anyway, but through an immature metaphysical perspective. As a result of such a separation, therefore, no one will suffer more than psychologists—and, through them, psychology. If philosophers now complain, unjustifiably, that psychology has become merely a technical rather than a purely scientific discipline, that would become even more—and more disturbingly—the case . . . and then the time truly will have been reached when psychologists will have made themselves into craftspeople (*Handwerker*), and, at that, not of the most useful variety.

(Wundt, 2013, p. 204)

Clearly, although Wundt did not believe in 1913 that psychology had already become "merely a technical" discipline, his position was that *if* psychology followed through on its wish to divorce from philosophy, that is exactly what psychology *would* become. That development, Wundt believed, would diminish rather than enhance psychology's status as a "purely scientific discipline" (*als eine reine wissenschaftliche Disziplin*; Wundt, 1913, p. 24), and would result in the discipline's degeneration into a merely technical discipline—a kind of craft union. In other words, a psychology indifferent to—or, worse yet, contemptuous of—the conceptual contributions of philosophically minded thinkers would ultimately lose its struggle for existence, its *Kampf ums Dasein*, as a genuine science.

Had Wundt's urgings regarding psychology's pending divorce from philosophy been more widely heeded, it seems unlikely that psychology would have become as hospitable as it did (and is) to scientism. In turn, the conceptual problems to which the field has fallen prey, such as those highlighted in the other chapters of this volume, might well have been minimized if not avoided altogether. This is not how things unfolded, however, and the conceit of the present volume is that psychology continues to be crippled by the untoward consequences of that development.

One prominent contemporary of Wundt who made explicit his alliance with Wundt's views on this matter was William Stern (1871–1938). Consider, for example, the striking similarity between the just quoted passage from Wundt (2013) and the following passage, written by Stern more than two decades later:

The separation of two independent approaches—the metaphysical and the empirical—is no more possible within scientific psychology than in lay psychology or artistic psychology. On the contrary, a symbiotic relationship between philosophical considerations and methodological findings is unavoidably necessary. The conviction, still now widespread, that psychology could or should become a discipline fully independent of philosophy leads either to a psychology without a psyche or to scientific work that incorporates a world view and grounding epistemological presuppositions that are not consciously recognized.

(Stern, 1935, p. 10)[9]

Nor can it properly be said that Stern arrived at this view only late in his scholarly life. On the contrary, as the author of a comprehensive system of thought (a *Weltanschauung* or 'worldview') that he called "critical personalism," Stern wrote in the first of his three-volume exposition of that framework, published 7 years prior to Wundt's 1913 essay, the following:

One ought not to think that the system of thought that I call 'critical personalism' has been shaped by my engagements in the domain of scientific psychology. On the contrary: I oppose psychologism, [a view that] would subordinate metaphysical considerations, which are simultaneously meta-psychological, to the science of consciousness.

(Stern, 1906, p. viii, brackets added)

In what follows, further attention will be given to Stern's contributions in the domain of differential psychology because they are, in ways to be shown, of historical relevance in the rise of an especially pernicious form of scientism that I have labeled 'statisticism'. I think it arguable that statisticism is the single most widespread and problematic form of scientism present in psychology today.

William Stern, Differential Psychology, and the Roots of Statisticism in Psychological Research

In his *A History of Civilization in England*, first published in 1857, Henry Thomas Buckle (1821–1862) wrote: "[From carefully compiled statistical facts] more may be learned [about] the moral nature of Man than can be gathered from all the accumulated experiences of the preceding ages" (Buckle, 1898, p. 17). In a 2013 publication (Lamiell, 2013b), I suggested the term 'statisticism' to characterize a way of thinking in psychology that invests virtually boundless trust in the aptness of statistical concepts and methods to reveal the 'lawfulness' in—and hence scientifically true nature of—human psychological functioning. For an elaboration of the essential spirit of statisticism, one could scarcely do better than these words by Buckle.

Intriguingly, the original publication of Buckle's work preceded the opening of Wundt's laboratory by more than two decades. Buckle's beliefs notwithstanding, however, experimental psychology did not, at its founding, employ the statistical methods of which Buckle was so enamored.[10] On the contrary, it was only with the establishment of a 'differential' psychology, primarily through the efforts of Stern, that such methods would find a place in the discipline's methodological toolbox.

As Stern pointed out in his 1900 book, titled (in translation) *On the Psychology of Individual Differences: Toward a "Differential Psychology"* (Stern, 1900), Wundtian experimental psychology was systematically uninterested in empirical manifestations of human individuality. That psychology was concerned exclusively with the quest for scientific knowledge of the laws governing aspects of the consciousness of human beings *in general*, where 'general' was understood in a way that meant *common to all*.[11] While Stern did not deem this an unworthy scientific objective, he did believe that in order for scientific psychology to survive moving forward, it would have to find a way to accommodate manifestations of human individuality as well, and he argued that the establishment of a subdiscipline of psychology specifically devoted to the study of the *differences between* individuals (and groups) would be an important step in this direction. Clearly, where systematic individual differences could be found in some domain of psychological functioning, claims to knowledge of a lawfulness 'common to all' would be *contra*indicated, and this would open the door to further consideration of the individuality of psychological functioning in that domain. This was the basic idea that Stern introduced in his 1900 book, and it was to an extension of that proposition that he devoted his second book on differential psychology, titled (in translation) *Methodological Foundations of Differential Psychology* (Stern, 1911).

In a retrospective on these developments published in 1913, Stern explained that the original single-subject approach to experimental research established through the Wundtian model (cf. Danziger, 1990) had to be modified in such a way as to make possible "the study of more complex behaviors and characteristics . . . [To] this end, survey procedures and methods of statistical analysis made their way into our discipline" (Stern, 1914, p. 416). Here we find Stern explicitly designating differential psychology as the portal through which the systematic consideration of population-level statistical knowledge entered scientific psychology. Within this newly established subdiscipline, intelligence testing and all other forms of psychological testing would be situated and virtually define that branch of psychological inquiry that Cronbach would, several decades later, call "correlational" psychology (Cronbach, 1957). Yet while Stern himself would make major contributions in the domain of psychological testing (cf. Lamiell, 2010), he never believed that the study of individual and group differences could, even in principle, lead to a satisfactory understanding of human individualities. He clearly stated his convictions in this regard in the 1900 book (cf. Lamiell, 2003), and he sought to institutionalize those convictions within differential psychology more formally and emphatically in the 1911 volume.

In the latter work, Stern laid out four research schemes that, together, would make up the differential psychology. Two of those schemes would entail the study of many individuals simultaneously, focusing either on a single variable (e.g., intelligence, sociability, conscientiousness), a scheme for inquiry that Stern called "variation" research; or on two or more such variables studied simultaneously to discover their interrelationships, a scheme for inquiry that Stern called "correlational" research. Stern emphasized the importance of understanding both of those research schemes as yielding knowledge of *variables*, with individuals serving merely as 'placeholders' occupying the different positions along the scales being used to represent those variables empirically.

It would be with the framework of the other two research schemes, Stern maintained, that knowledge about individualities would be generated. One of those two schemes, called "psychography," would entail the study of a single individual in terms of multiple attributes, while the other scheme, called "comparison" research, could be used to juxtapose the psychographic profiles of two or more individuals for purposes of determining their similarities and differences.

In all of this, Stern's conviction was firm that studies of variables with respect to which individuals have been differentiated is neither equivalent to nor substitutable for studies of the individuals who have been differentiated in terms of those variables. It is this basic epistemological point that would be lost on—or simply ignored by—other prominent differential psychologists of Stern's time, and these latter are the ones who proved to be most influential.

One very important consequence of this conflation was the previously discussed confusion among latter-day personality psychologists about the meaning of the correlation coefficients they were so fervently examining with respect to the question of (in)consistency in the behavioral manifestations by individuals of their respective personality traits.

An early and particularly egregious example of this confusion appeared in a monograph published by E.L. Thorndike (1874–1949) in 1911, titled *Individuality*.[12] In that work, Thorndike elaborated the meaning of a correlation between two trait variables "in a collection of individuals" as indicating "the extent to which the amount of one trait possessed *by an individual* is bound up with the amount *he* possesses of some other trait" (Thorndike, 1911, p. 21, emphasis added). Although Thorndike did not state explicitly what he meant by the phrase "bound up with," it is clear from context that he intended it to mean the degree of correspondence between an individual's respective standings on the two variables that had been correlated. On his view, then, knowledge of the correlation between two variables just *is*, at one and the same time, knowledge of the individuals who have been differentiated in terms of those two variables. If this were true, it would render superfluous the additional research schemes that Stern labeled "psychography" and "comparison" studies, and as an overall framework for psychological research, differential psychology would reduce from Stern's original four schemes to the two he labeled "variation" and "correlational." This is, in fact, exactly the way differential psychology developed in the 20th century (cf. Lamiell, 2003).

There is, however, a very basic conceptual problem here. The statement by Thorndike quoted earlier is *false*. From knowledge of the magnitude of a correlation between two variables defined for a collection of individuals (e.g., for a sample of size N taken from some population), it is most emphatically *not* possible to claim knowledge of the degree of correspondence in *any* one individual's respective standings on those two variables.[13] Any correlation of the sort discussed by Thorndike (1911) is, just as Stern (1911) had insisted, knowledge of the *variables* under consideration, and *not* knowledge of any of the individuals who have been differentiated in terms of those variables. Put succinctly, Stern (1911) was right and Thorndike (1911) was wrong. Had conceptual clarity throughout scientific psychology been insisted upon with respect to this and many other points bearing on the use of population-level statistics in the attempt to advancing our scientific understanding of individual-level psychological doings, specious knowledge claims of the sort that are now endemic might very well have been nipped in the bud.[14]

A Concluding Comment

Quite obviously, the conceptual clarity needed to correct Thorndike's (1911) misstatement was nowhere to be found.[15] Even worse, however, is the abiding obstinacy of mainstream thinkers in the face of repeated expositions of the conceptual flaws that infect their canonical research practices.[16] For the present, at least, it appears that that particular form of scientism that I have called 'statisticism' has rendered mainstream thinking incorrigible with respect to the essential nature of their own statistical research findings (Lamiell & Martin, 2017). Although space limitations preclude a further discussion of the matter here, this incorrigibility has serious consequences, both epistemic and ethical. In the epistemic domain, contemporary researchers customarily overstate what they may justifiably claim to *know* on the basis of their research findings. This is bad science. In the ethical domain, researchers customarily overstate what they may justifiably *do*, or endorse doing, under the banner of scientifically licensed interventions in various domains of human affairs. This is bad professional practice.

The longer mainstream psychologists continue to dismiss critiques of the sort offered here on the grounds that they are 'merely' conceptual and hence are of no real value to a genuinely scientific psychology, the closer they drive their discipline toward the fate Wundt predicted for it in 1913. That is, the *less* the discipline will qualify as a genuine science, dedicated to "the colligation of facts and the clarification of concepts," and the more it will become— one might even say, with Wundt, 'merely'—a kind of craft union, perhaps worthy as such in its own right, but hardly commensurate with its scientific pretensions.

Notes

1 The letter *r* is the commonly accepted symbol for the Pearson product-moment correlation coefficient, by far the most widely used index of correlation in the research literature of psychology.

2 For full explanation and vivid empirical illustration of this point, see Lamiell (1987, pp. 99–108).

3 The *only* exception to this would have been a *perfect* correlation (i.e., $r = 1.00$), and of course this logical possibility was never obtained empirically. Here again, the reader puzzled over this point should refer to Lamiell (1987, pp. 99–108).

4 These quoted phrases are from a 1989 republication of a work by Whewell (as cited in Machado & Silva, 2007, p. 680, emphasis added).

5 For my English translation of the entirety of this essay, see Wundt (2013). In what follows, all references to the essay, except where otherwise explicitly indicated, will be to the 2013 translation, and, likewise except where indicated, all quotations of the essay will be cited using page numbers from the 2013 translation.

6 In the essay, Wundt referred to this group as "*die reinen Philosophen*"; literally 'the pure philosophers'.

7 The reader should note in Wundt's wording, both here and further along in his essay (see below), the clear indication that he regarded philosophy as part of the domain of science (*Wissenschaft*). There was nothing at all peculiar about this at the time, although it would seem quite strange to most contemporaries. This itself is a legacy of scientism.

8 I find the commonly used expression 'abnormal psychology' rather infelicitous.

9 Here and throughout the remainder of this chapter, all translations from original German language works are the author's unless otherwise indicated.

10 To be sure, statistical calculations were sometimes employed, quite prominently, for example, in Hermann Ebbinghaus's famous experiments on memory (Ebbinghaus, 1885). However, all of the data on which Ebbinghaus based his calculations were associated with the same *one* experimental subject (who happened to be Ebbinghaus himself), and those calculations were carried out as a way of *estimating measurement error*. The statistical calculations of the sort to which Buckle (1857/1898) was referring were (and still are) carried out on observations made of *many* individuals sampled from populations, and the purpose of

38   *James T. Lamiell*

those calculations was (and is) to *estimate population-level parameters*, most commonly means, variances, and covariances. Epistemically speaking, these are two vastly different methods of procedure.

11 For psychology's first experimentalists, the expression 'true in general' emphatically did *not* mean 'true on average'. However, this latter—and vastly different—meaning *did* become the understanding of 'general' that research psychologists embraced once they adopted population-level statistical concepts and methods as a means of conducting their research. Alas, as this transformation unfolded there was a discipline-wide failure to grasp—or to scrupulously respect—the truth of the observation by the Leipzig philosopher and mathematician Moritz Wilhelm Drobisch (1802–1896) that "it is only through a great failure of understanding [that] the mathematical fiction of an average man . . . [can] be elaborated as if all individuals . . . possess a real part of whatever obtains for this average person" (Drobisch, 1867, quoted in Porter, 1986, p. 171). This great failure of understanding is the root of the problem of statisticism in contemporary psychological research.

12 It is ironic that this work by Thorndike appeared in the same year as did Stern's *Methodological Foundations of Differential Psychology*.

13 The same empirical illustration provided by Lamiell (1987) and referred to earlier suffices to illustrate this point, and the reader still uncertain about the validity of the point is strongly urged to consult that illustration.

14 The very same arguments, developed here within the context of correlational research, apply to the *treatment group* method of experimentation (Danziger, 1990) that came to displace Wundtian-style ($N = 1$) experimentation within mainstream psychology. For extended discussions of this point, see Lamiell (2015, 2016).

15 I should not leave the reader with the impression that Thorndike was single-handedly responsible for running differential psychology off the rails of conceptual clarity in this regard. Another very prominent and influential differential psychologist of the time, Hugo Münsterberg (1863–1916), shared Thorndike's views, a fact clearly reflected in his highly influential textbook *Psychology and Industrial Efficiency* (Münsterberg, 1913). Consider, for example, Münsterberg's discussion of correlational findings he had uncovered in his studies of individual differences in attention:

> We found that typical connections exist between apparently independent features of attention. Persons who have a rather expansive span of attention for acoustical impressions have also a wide span for the visual objects . . . Hence the manifestation (by a person) of one feature of attention allows us to presuppose without further tests that certain other features may be expected *in the particular individual*.
> (Münsterberg, 1913, pp. 135–136, parentheses and emphasis added)

So just as did Thorndike, Münsterberg adopted the view that a correlation between two variables marking *individual differences* in some psychological domain (in this case, attention) is a scientifically sound basis for inferring the degree of correspondence in the respective standings of some *individual* on those two variables. It has proven extremely difficult—nay, impossible to date—to disabuse differential psychologists of the validity of this notion (cf. Lamiell, 2007).

16 For vivid examples of alternative research practices that are not subject to those same conceptual flaws, see, e.g., Grice (2011); Grice et al. (2006, 2012, 2015); Molenaar (2004).

References

Ash, M. (1980). Wilhelm Wundt and Oswald Külpe on the institutional status of psychology: An academic controversy in historical context. In W.G. Bringmann & R.D. Tweney (Eds.), *Wundt studies* (pp. 396–421). Toronto, ON: C.J. Hogrefe.

Bem, D.J., & Allen, A. (1974). On predicting some of the people some of the time: The search for cross-situational consistencies in behavior. *Psychological Review*, *81*, 506–520.

Bem, D.J., & Funder, D.C. (1978). Predicting more of the people more of the time: Assessing the personality of situations. *Psychological Review*, *85*, 485–501.

Block, J. (1977). Advancing the psychology of personality: Paradigmatic shift or improving the quality of research? In D. Magnusson & N.S. Endler (Eds.), *Personality at the crossroads: Current issues in interactional psychology* (pp. 37–68). Hillsdale, NJ: Erlbaum.

Buckle, H.T. (1898). *A history of civilization in England*. New York: D. Appleton. (Original work published 1857)

Cronbach, L.J. (1957). The two disciplines of scientific psychology. *American Psychologist*, *12*, 671–684.

Danziger, K. (1990). *Constructing the subject: Historical origins of psychological research*. New York: Cambridge University Press.

Ebbinghaus, H. (1885). *Über das Gedächtnis* [On memory]. Leipzig, Germany: Verlag von Duncker and Humbolt.

Epstein, S. (1977). Traits are alive and well. In D. Magnusson & N.S. Endler (Eds.), *Personality at the crossroads: Current issues in interactional psychology* (pp. 83–98). Hillsdale, NJ: Erlbaum.

Epstein, S. (1979). The stability of behavior, I: On predicting most of the people much of the time. *Journal of Personality and Social Psychology*, *37*, 1097–1126.

Epstein, S. (1980). The stability of behavior, II: Implications for psychological research. *American Psychologist*, *35*, 790–806.

Epstein, S. (1983). Aggregation and beyond: Some basic issues in the prediction of behavior. *Journal of Personality*, *51*, 360–392.

Grice, J.W. (2011). *Observation oriented modeling: Analysis of cause in the behavioral sciences*. New York: Academic Press.

Grice, J.W., Barrett, P.T., Schlimgen, L.A., & Abramson, C.I. (2012). Toward a brighter future for psychology as an observation oriented science. *Behavioral Science*, *2*, 1–22.

Grice, J.W., Cohn, A., Ramsey, R.R., & Chaney, J.M. (2015). On muddled reasoning and mediation modeling. *Basic and Applied Social Psychology*, *37*, 214–225.

Grice, J.W., Jackson, B.J., & McDaniel, B.L. (2006). Bridging the idiographic-nomothetic divide: A follow-up study. *Journal of Personality*, *74*, 1191–1218.

Jüttemann, G. (Ed.). (2006). *Wilhelm Wundts anderes Erbe: Ein missverständnis löst sich auf* [Wundt's other legacy: The resolution of a misunderstanding]. Göttingen, Germany: Vandenhoeck & Ruprecht.

Lamiell, J.T. (1981). Toward an idiothetic psychology of personality. *American Psychologist*, *36*, 276–289.

Lamiell, J.T. (1987). *The psychology of personality: An epistemological inquiry*. New York: Columbia University Press.

Lamiell, J.T. (2003). *Beyond individual and group differences: Human individuality, scientific psychology, and William Stern's critical personalism.* Thousand Oaks, CA: Sage.

Lamiell, J.T. (2007). On sustaining critical discourse with mainstream personality investigators: Problems and prospects. *Theory and Psychology, 17,* 169–185.

Lamiell, J.T. (2010). *William Stern (1871–1938): A brief introduction to his life and works.* Lengerich, Germany: Pabst Science.

Lamiell, J.T. (2013a). On psychology's struggle for existence: Some reflections on Wundt's 1913 essay a century on. *Journal of Theoretical and Philosophical Psychology, 33,* 205–215.

Lamiell, J.T. (2013b). Statisticism in personality psychologists' use of trait constructs: What is it? How was it contracted? Is there a cure? *New Ideas in Psychology, 31,* 65–71.

Lamiell, J.T. (2015). Statistical thinking in psychological research: In quest of clarity through historical inquiry and conceptual analysis. In J. Martin, J. Sugarman, & K.L. Slaney (Eds.), *The Wiley handbook of theoretical and philosophical psychology: Methods, approaches, and new directions for social sciences* (pp. 200–215). Hoboken, NJ: John Wiley and Sons.

Lamiell, J.T. (2016). On the concept of "effects" in contemporary psychological experimentation: A case study in the need for conceptual clarity and discursive precision. In R. Harré & F. Moghaddam (Eds.), *Questioning causality: Scientific explorations of cause and consequence across social contexts* (pp. 83–102). Santa Barbara, CA: Praeger.

Lamiell, J.T., & Martin, J. (2017). The incorrigible science. In H. Macdonald, D. Goodman, & B. Decker (Eds.), *Dialogues at the edge of American psychological discourse: Critical and theoretical perspectives in psychology* (pp. 211–244). London: Palgrave Macmillan.

Machado, A., & Silva, F.J. (2007). Toward a richer view of the scientific method: The role of conceptual analysis. *American Psychologist, 62,* 671–681.

Mischel, W. (1968). *Personality and assessment.* New York: Wiley.

Molenaar, P.C.M. (2004). A manifesto on psychology as idiographic science: Bringing the person back into scientific psychology, this time forever. *Measurement, 2,* 201–218.

Münsterberg, H. (1913). *Psychology and industrial efficiency.* Boston, MA: Houghton Mifflin.

Porter, T.M. (1986). *The rise of statistical thinking: 1820–1900.* Princeton, NJ: Princeton University Press.

Stern, W. (1900). *Über Psychologie der individuellen Differenzen (Ideen zu einer differentiellen Psychologie)* [On the psychology of individual differences: Toward a differential psychology]. Leipzig: Barth.

Stern, W. (1906). *Person und Sache: System der philosophischen Weltanschauung, erster Band: Ableitung und Grundlehre* [Person and thing: A systematic philosophical worldview, Volume 1: Rationale and basic tenets]. Leipzig: Barth.

Stern, W. (1911). *Die differentielle Psychologie in ihren methodologischen Grundlagen* [Methodological foundations of differential psychology]. Leipzig: Barth.

Stern, W. (1914). Psychologie [Psychology]. In D. Sarason (Ed.), *Das Jahr 1913: Ein Gesamtbild der Kulturentwicklung* (pp. 414–421). Leipzig: Teubner.

Stern, W. (1935). *Allgemeine Psychologie auf personalistischer Grundlage* [General psychology from a personalistic standpoint]. The Hague: Martinus Nijhoff.

Thorndike, E. L. (1911). *Individuality*. New York: Houghton Mifflin.

Wundt, W. (1913). *Die Psychologie im Kampf ums Dasein* (2nd ed.). Leipzig: Kröner.

Wundt, W. (2013). Psychology's struggle for existence (J. T. Lamiell, Trans.). *History of Psychology*, *16*, 195–209.

4   Why Science Needs Intuition

Lisa M. Osbeck

Introduction: Science Against Intuition

The dichotomizing habits of human thinking incline us toward conceptual inaccuracies, one of which is a fairly long-standing tendency to regard science and scientific reasoning as in antagonistic relation to the realm of all that is mysterious, irreducible, spiritual, emotionally engaging, or poetic. But this tendency can be seen to be of relatively recent origin when viewed in broader historical context. Danziger acknowledges a "great transformation" beginning in the latter part of the 18th century and continuing into the 19th, whereby

> two kinds of knowledge came to be more and more sharply distinguished: one based on the distanced, dispassionate observation of nature encouraged by science, the other typified by the more subjective, involved, way of expressed in the new literary and artistic style of Romanticism.
>
> (Danziger, 1997, p. 49)

"Science writes of the world as if with the cold finger of a starfish, *but what is it when compared to the reality of which it discourses?*" laments Robert Louis Stevenson in *Pan's Pipes* (1906, p. 279), reflecting entrenchment of a myth of separation between intellect and passion—a separation upheld by both scientist and poet, and never more so than in the 19th century (Dror, 2009). A more contemporary version of this myth of separation supported narratives of clinical decision making that pitted a murky and unreliable clinical 'intuition' against the precision of actuarial or statistical methods of prediction (e.g., Meehl, 1954).

Some philosophers of science, most notably Polanyi (1974), have challenged a view of science as disengaged and provide critical revisions of the role of scientific passions. Cognitive science increasingly features a complex, entangled relation between emotional and cognitive processes, and inclines toward underscoring the beneficial contribution of emotion to rational decision making (Bechara, 2004; Damasio, 2003; De Sousa, 2001; Haidt, 2007; Magnani, 2017; McAllister, 2005; Nussbaum, 2001; Thagard, 2008). Similarly, 'values', once condemned to the realm of furtive subjectivity and thus out of step with the project of objectivity, have now been viewed, for several decades at least, as inextricable from and even advantageous to science (Douglas, 2009; Lauden, 1984; Longino, 1990). However, 'intuition' has not enjoyed quite the same rethinking in relation to the projects and purposes of scientific reasoning. Famously, Einstein, Poincaré, and Feynman extolled intuition's importance in discovery, primarily in conversations and interviews, but what they intended by intuition has never been entirely clear.

The elusive nature of any concept of intuition offers affordances of various kinds, one of which, in recent years, is commercial commodification: at present a cologne, razor, vacuum cleaner, microbrew, cellular phone, software development company, and aromatherapy products all bear a product name of 'intuition'. In addition, a "cottage industry" (Myers, 2002) of self-styled 'intuitives' has emerged to provide guidance toward personal knowledge, enhanced effectiveness, physical and mental healing, and spiritual growth. Although amusing from a certain point of view, commercial exploitations of what has long been acknowledged as a highly ambiguous concept detract from serious consideration of the implications of the prominent role intuition has played in many philosophical traditions, including those for which an account of the possibility of scientific knowledge is a central aim and achievement. I suggest that there are several important but distinct senses in which a notion of intuition bears an important relation to science; that is, that may be considered necessary to science in various ways. As I will discuss, some notion of intuition is exploited in relation to intuitive contact with objects, the development of scientific concepts, the organization or arrangements of concepts, and the condition of possibility of the empirical (i.e., experience itself) in various philosophical contexts. At stake are different forms, senses, or conceptions of intuition; what is required is historically informed philosophical analysis of phenomena variably translated as intuition to make these clear. Analysis of the various functions intuitions serve in the contexts in question will help not only in the general project of conceptual clarity; it will also help to inform our understanding of scientific reasoning in the requisite richness by which it has been understood historically.

Intuition *in* Science

Given the space constraints of this chapter, I have time to provide only a brief survey of some of the relevant contexts and forms of intuition invoked, and also to give only a cursory analysis of any similarities that might be suggested by their comparison.

As a general overview, intuition appears historically as a special sort of cognitive or intellectual act, a privileged form of apprehension by means of which the mind transcends sensory channels to gain understandings of a privileged kind. Intuition is best understood as 'immediate apprehension', with 'immediate' understood as 'without mediation', implying without interference or supplementation from other processes—direct. Intuitive knowledge, the product of this apprehension, is distinguished by its pivotal role in establishing a means by which knowledge claims may be justified. That we are advantaged with direct apprehension of *some* kind is generally accepted by Scholastic philosophers, in discussions that are pivotally important to the establishment of modern scientific method. What is debated is the *form* of knowledge we apprehend directly, specifically, whether common qualities (universals), relations, or particular existent things, with what degree of necessity, and in what proportion. It is the special feature of immediacy or directness that functions to secure some kind of bedrock or foundation for knowledge claims, even if philosophers have disagreed on the source and degree of security of that foundation. Differences in accounts of what is intuited, that is, apprehended directly impact the extent to which the objects of the intuitive faculty are to be taken as establishing certain, even indubitable knowledge in some cases (e.g., Descartes, *De Regulae*, 1994/1628), or whether they remain merely contingently true, subject to disconfirmation in experience.

(1) Intuitive Apprehension of Objects

One very basic way in which intuition is construed as necessary to science is as the means by which we achieve contact with or awareness of the world: the very grounds of possibility of action, and the basis for explicit propositions about the objects of which we become aware, such that they can be tested in experience. Although very broadly corresponding to a form of intuition labeled "sensory intuition" by later philosophers (e.g., Rorty, 1967), models of how intuitive contact occurs are variable. However it occurs, the process is not reducible *to* sensation, but accompanies sensation and is inseparable from it. This is very clearly illustrated in William of Ockham's (1287–1347) view that intuition provides immediate awareness of things, of particulars. Things themselves, objects in the world (that is, in this context, anything with dimension), are directly given or presented to awareness through intuition. We could say that intuitions are produced by things themselves, but this is so by virtue of their relation to the cognizer's active perceptual powers. Intuition of particulars is a resonance with things—a subpropositional "intuitive contact" with the world, in Ockham scholar Claude Pannacio's phrasing (Pannacio, 2014, p. 70). We might see it as similar in this regard to the contemporary concept of 'embeddedness' of thought. It is an 'act of awareness' that is not sensation itself but is concurrent with sensation; it is not a matter of inference or conjecture. This immediate awareness then provides a grounding for propositions about the things intuited, including their qualities and relation to other things, which must be tested in experience. The intuition, that is, is the active grasping, but what it produces or evokes might be called a representation, trace, or modification in the psyche in the presence of the object.

For Ockham, because only individual things are intuited, general terms (concepts) cannot be predicated of any object by necessity. Although scientific propositions have universals or general ideas as subject terms, the universals stand for aggregates of individuals, because these are all we know. Scientific concepts are based on the fact of repetition of similar features, not from any inherent nature or essence. Thus, concepts are merely constructions on this view (see Pannacio for in-depth treatment of Ockham's position of concepts).

(2) Intuitive Origin of General Ideas (Scientific Concepts)

However, for other philosophers, including Aristotle and those, like Aquinas, who are principally informed by him, it is principally the universal or common quality that is actively grasped through intuition. Aristotle's distinction between primary and secondary substance, and the related idea of accidental and essential properties of things, reflects the awareness that the properties, the features of 'things' or particulars, undergo transformations. Essential properties are those that amount to the definitive characteristics or nature that make an object the sort of thing that it is, without which it would not be a thing of that kind. For Aristotle, the essence is more than the qualities of appearance but is the end or purpose of the existing thing, its identifying function. The essence or function of an object is known in a different way than is knowledge of the changeable, accidental set of qualities bound to the object's appearance. Although enabled by sense perception, knowledge of essential qualities is an accomplishment of the intellect, made possible through an active, intuitive grasp. For Aquinas too, it is the task of the agent intellect to abstract the universal idea from the experiential contact with individual objects, thereby making them open to understanding. On this view the intuitive grasp of universals is assumed to hearken back to *a priori* structures, that is, the world as it is. Nevertheless, note that whether universals *or* particulars are the objects of intuitive acts was a matter subjected to debate in Scholastic philosophy, not *that* we rely on intuitive acts to ground our knowledge, and not *whether* sensation and intellectual cognition are cooperatively employed in the pursuit of knowledge of causes and principles that correspond to the structure of nature. It was assumed that we do and that they are (Jardine, 1974).

(3) Intuitive Grasp of Relations Between General Ideas (Organization of Concepts)

Whatever their origin, science requires more than the formation of general ideas or concepts; it requires understanding of *relations* between concepts. Relations between ideas are also matters that have been conceptualized as intuitively grasped. Certainly, the view that necessary relations are intuited— and thus provide a basis for logic and mathematical reasoning—is central to the epistemological projects of Plato, Aristotle, and their philosophical offspring, with the grasp of necessary relations frequently labeled "rational intuition" to distinguish it from the tradition of sensory intuition already discussed. For Descartes, intuition is necessary "to provide a method for ordering one's investigations, regardless of the domain" (Machamer & Adams, 2014). The queenly science of mathematics, with the clarity and distinctness by which mathematical relations are apprehended, becomes a model for the method that will, as Descartes puts it, enable one to "increase the natural light of (his) reason" (*De Regulae* AT X.368). This "natural light" is, in the early Descartes, at least, instantiated in the cooperative intellectual acts of intuition and deduction, with intuition analogized to ordinary vision by means of the Latin verb used, *intueri*, which translates as 'to look to' or 'to look at' (Cottingham, 1994), meaning 'immediately evident' or 'right away apparent'. Descartes in this work affirms that the grasp of necessary relations is always intuitive, and that it is this intuitive grasp that grounds deductive certainty. He calls intuition "a single and distinct act which is similar in every case" (*De Regulae* IX, 401). This, in turn, provides a foundation for the possibility of deductive science. He notes: "Very many facts which are not self-evident are known with certainty, provided they are inferred from true and known principles through a continuous and uninterrupted movement of thought in which each individual proposition is clearly intuited" (*De Regulae* III, 369).

It might be noted, too, that the empiricist Locke, although he rejects any doctrine of innate ideas, nevertheless preserves as a "rational power" the "perception of the connextion [*sic*] and agreement, or disagreement and repugnancy of any of our ideas" (Locke, *Essay* IV, I, 2). The connection between ideas is apprehended or perceived in varying degrees of immediacy, strength, or certainty. Intuitive knowledge is the awareness of relationships between ideas to such a degree of certainty that eliminates doubt: "it is on this intuition that depends all the certainty and evidence of all our knowledge" (*Essay* IV, I, 4). Locke similarly considers intuition so understood to play a role in demonstrative knowledge or deduction, including mathematical proofs.

(4) Condition of Possibility of Experience

In what might be regarded as concern with a more profound level of organization of our scientific concepts, Kant relies on a notion of intuition to establish the conditions that determine the possibility of experience itself. Kant establishes intuition as something like the organizing principle that makes experience possible, the very precondition of experience. This is grounded in a very difficult formulation of the synthetic *a priori*, which is beyond the scope of this brief chapter but, very roughly, features the following assumptions critical to our purposes: Objects are given by intuition and represented through the active generation of conceptions, identified with understanding. Both conception and intuition may be pure or impure, with pure understood as devoid of empirical content, that is, of experience. Kant calls "empirical intuitions" "that sort of intuition which relates to an object by means of sensation" (*Critique*, Elements, Introduction, p. 21), but Kant further specifies that "that which effects that the content of the phenomenon can be arranged under certain conditions"—that is, its form cannot be given in sensation. Therefore, "we find existing in the mind, a priori, the pure forms of sensuous intuitions in general, in which the manifold content of the phenomenal world is arranged under certain relations. . . . this pure form of sensibility I call pure intuition" (*Critique* Elements, I, Introduction, 1990, p. 22). The two pure forms so described are space and time. Space is "the condition of the possibility of phenomena . . . which necessarily supplies the basis for external phenomena" (1990, p. 24). As a pure intuition, "an a priori intuition (and pure, not empirical) lies at the root of all our conceptions of space," which includes the principles of geometry. Time is likewise "a necessary representation, lying at the foundation of all our intuitions." Time "is nothing else than the form of the internal sense, that is of the intuitions of self and our internal state . . . the formal condition a priori of all phenomena whatsoever" (*Critique*, Elements, I, 2, 1990, p. 30).

Kant thereby extends the notion of sensory intuition to include the means by which knowledge through the senses is made possible at all. In so doing he attributes form (space and time) to what had been considered unanalyzable. He also associates intuition with an *a priori* framework that establishes the conditions of understanding. By thus crediting intuition with the basis upon which experience (that is, the empirical) is possible, 'pure' intuition is in a sense more epistemologically fundamental than any other sense of intuition we have examined.

Intuition in Psychology

Intuition, despite its Enlightenment-era status as an intellectual act recognizable in consciousness in (for example, for Descartes, as clear and distinct perception), appears to have changed its conceptual contours over time, and now is most frequently encountered in connection with 'nonrational' cognitive processes, and as 'natural' in distinctions that construe scientific rationality as in some sense unnatural or artificial. This association between intuition and that which is in opposition to rational, deliberative judgment is evident in psychology's two-process models of cognition that contrast automatic with deliberative processing and include 'the intuitive' among the features of the automatic or nonrational system (Reber, 1993; Evans, 2010; Smith & Collins, 2009; Kahneman, 2011).

There is no clear story about how the transition in conceptualizing intuition took place or how this was facilitated by psychology. However, by the time of publication of Paul Meehl's influential work, *Clinical Versus Statistical Prediction: A Theoretical Analysis and a Review of the Evidence*, published in 1954, a clear dichotomy has been drawn. Although in this work Meehl famously disparaged what he called "clinical intuition" in comparison to "actuarial formulations," he later acknowledged that "some" clinical situations, with the psychoanalytic hour serving as a model, call for a "richness and subtlety" of judgment not obtainable with actuarial methods (Meehl, 1986, p. 372). Following Meehl, the project quickly shifted to that of evaluating the possibilities for conceiving "modes of information combination in tandem" and to understanding the means by which intuitive judgment and actuarial formula are used depending on the demands of the situation (Kleinmuntz, 1990).

The interest in a more integrative approach to the 'two-process' model has in recent years contributed to a renewed appreciation for the role of intuition in strategic reasoning and expertise, although there remains an assumed contrast with processes designated as deliberative and rational. It is now, at least, acknowledged that these other murkier processes play a role in facilitating adaptation to complex environments and in guiding us toward good decisions (Gigerenzer, 2000, 2007; Kahneman, 2011). Moreover, on the basis of enhanced imaging techniques, more elaborate or multisystem models have been proposed as alternatives in recent years (e.g., Kable & Glimcher, 2009), requiring, for example, new distinctions between processes previously collapsed, such as intuition and implicit memory (e.g., Volz & Zander, 2014). Although there have been few explicit analyses of the role of intuition in scientific reasoning per se, even in these contexts, the application to science seems a likely eventual extension of the recent turn to better understand the role of 'subjective' and nonrational processes (e.g., emotion and values) in scientific problem solving—an outgrowth of the 'affective revolution' in cognitive science (Haidt, 2007).

Conclusion

There is a deeply rooted contrast held at least implicitly by both the scientific community and by those concerned about its too-ambitious reach—a contrast between 'objective' knowledge gained through systematic observation and rigorous test, and the sometimes shadowy but sumptuous awareness obtained through subjective exploration.[1] Similarly, there is both a popular and scholarly tradition by which 'rational' processes are relegated to the former and 'intuition' to the latter. Yet the assumption of contrast between rationality and intuition rests upon specific and historically contingent understandings of objectivity, subjectivity, science, and intuition, and these are of relatively recent (19th century) origin (e.g., see Daston & Galison, 2007). In this chapter I have examined several earlier philosophical contexts in which some notion of intuition is invoked to serve purposes that are central to the very possibility of empirical knowledge, that is, to science itself: the presentation of empirical objects (connection to world); the formation of concepts; the organization or relation of concepts; the recognition of conditions of necessity, or law; and the very possibility of experience. Important about the analysis undertaken is that it points to the fundamental role of some form of 'direct' apprehension in the intellective acts that constitute (scientific) rationality, at least as these were understood in the broad historical and Western context examined here. These philosophical contexts remind us of an inescapable element of mystery, a 'directness' of apprehension beyond the powers of further reductive analysis—a mysterious aspect to our rational powers in which the very possibility of science is grounded. An elusive 'directness' in historical accounts of scientific reasoning may be understood not so much as a form of limit on the role and reach of science but as a limit on our ability to understand its very nature.

Note

1 Although there are interesting recent empirical studies of intuition, including neurological, the senses and functions of intuition and their relation to scientific reasoning are not matters that can be addressed through imaging studies, except as they help to illuminate the material grounding of processes that have been understood and articulated philosophically.

References

Bechara, A. (2004). The role of emotion in decision-making: Evidence from neurological patients with orbitofrontal damage. *Brain and Cognition, 55*(1), 30–40.

Cottingham, J. (Ed.). (1994). *Reason, will, and sensation: Studies in Descartes' Metaphysics.* Oxford, UK: Clarendon Press.

Damasio, A. R. (2003). *Looking for Spinoza: Joy, sorrow, and the feeling brain.* New York: Harcourt.

Danziger, K. (1997). *Naming the mind: How psychology found its language.* Thousand Oaks, CA: Sage.

Daston, L., & Galison, P. (2007). *Objectivity.* Cambridge, MA: MIT Press.

Descartes, R. (1994). Rules for the direction of the mind (*Regulae ad directionem ingenii*). In *Descartes: Selected philosophical writings* (J. Cottingham, R. Stoothoff, & D. Murdoch, Trans.). Cambridge: Cambridge University Press. (Original work published 1684; assumed written 1628)

De Sousa, R. (2001). *The rationality of emotion.* Cambridge, MA: MIT Press.

Douglas, H. (2009). *Science, policy, and the value-free ideal.* Pittsburgh, PA: University of Pittsburgh Press.

Dror, I. E. (2009). How can Francis Bacon help forensic science? The four idols of human biases. *Jurimetrics: The Journal of Law, Science, and Technology, 50,* 93–110.

Evans, J.S.B. (2010). Intuition and reasoning: A dual-process perspective. *Psychological Inquiry, 21*(4), 313–326.

Gigerenzer, G. (2000). *Adaptive thinking: Rationality in the real world.* Oxford: Oxford University Press.

Gigerenzer, G. (2007). *Gut feelings. The intelligence of the unconscious.* New York: Viking Penguin.

Haidt, J. (2007). The new synthesis in moral psychology. *Science, 18*(31), 998–1002.

Kable, J. W., & Glimcher, P. W. (2009). The neurobiology of decision: Consensus and controversy. *Neuron, 63*(6), 733–745.

Kahneman, D. (2011). *Thinking fast and slow.* New York: Palgrave Macmillan.

Kant, I. (1990). *Critique of pure reason* (J.M.D. Meidlejohn, Trans.). Buffalo, NY: Prometheus. (Original work published 1781)

Kleinmuntz, B. (1990). Why we still use our heads instead of formulas: Toward an integrative approach. *Psychological Bulletin, 107,* 296.

Jardine, L. (1974). *Francis Bacon: Discovery and the art of discourse.* Cambridge: Cambridge University Press.

Lauden, L. (1984). *Science and values: The aims of science and their role in scientific debate.* Berkeley: University of California Press.

Longino, H. (1990). *Science as social knowledge: Values and objectivity in scientific inquiry.* Princeton, NJ: Princeton University Press.

Locke, J. (1964). *An essay concerning human understanding.* New York: William Collins. (Original work published 1690)

Machamer, P., & Adams, M. (2014). Descartes on intuition and ideas. In L. Osbeck & B. Held (Eds.), *Rational intuition* (pp. 75–89). New York: Cambridge University Press.

Magnani, L. (2017). *The abductive structure of scientific creativity: An essay on the ecology of cognition.* Cham, Switzerland: Springer.

McAllister, J. W. (2005). Emotion, rationality, and decision making in science. In P. Hájek, L. Valdés-Villanueva, & D. Westerståhl (Eds.), *Logic, methodology and philosophy of science: Proceedings of the Twelfth International Congress* (pp. 559–576). London: King's College.

Meehl, P. E. (1954). *Clinical versus statistical prediction: A theoretical analysis and review of the literature.* Minneapolis: University of Minnesota Press.

Meehl, P. E. (1986). Causes and effects of my disturbing little book. *Journal of Personality Assessment, 50*(3), 370–375.

Myers, D. G. (2002). *Intuition: Its powers and perils.* New Haven, CT: Yale University Press.

Nussbaum, M. C. (2001). *Upheavals of thought: The intelligence of emotions.* Cambridge: Cambridge University Press.

Pannacio, C. (2014). Ockham: Intuition and knowledge. In L. Osbeck & B. Held (Eds.), *Rational intuition: Philosophical roots, scientific investigations.* New York: Cambridge University Press.

Pannacio, C. (2017). *Ockham on concepts.* New York: Routledge.

Polanyi, M. (1974). *Personal knowledge: Towards a post-critical philosophy.* Chicago, IL: University of Chicago Press. (Original work published 1958)

Reber, A. S. (1993). *Oxford psychology series, No. 19: Implicit learning and tacit knowledge: An essay on the cognitive unconscious.* New York: Oxford University Press.

Rorty, R. (1967). Intuition. *Encyclopedia of Philosophy, 3,* 204–212.

Smith, E. R., & Collins, E. C. (2009). Dual-process models: A social psychological perspective. In J. Evans & K. Frankish (Eds.), *In two minds: Dual processes and beyond* (pp. 197–216). Oxford: Oxford University Press.

Stevenson, R. L. (1906). Pan's pipes. In C. Bigelow & C. Scott (Eds.), *The works of Robert Louis Stevenson* (Vol. 6, pp. 76–79). New York: Davos Press.

Thagard, P. (2008). *Hot thought.* Cambridge, MA: MIT Press.

Volz, K. G., & Zander, T. (2014). Primed for intuition? *Neuroscience of Decision Making, 1,* 26–34.

5 Scientism and Saturation

Evolutionary Psychology, Human Experience, and the Phenomenology of Jean-Luc Marion

Edwin E. Gantt

> If the natural sciences had been developed in Socrates's day as they are now all the sophists would have been scientists. One would have hung a microscope outside his shop in order to attract custom, and then would have had a sign painted saying: "Learn and see through a giant microscope how a man thinks" (and on reading the advertisement Socrates would have said: "that is how men who do not think think").
>
> —Søren Kierkegaard[1]

The philosopher of science, Wilfrid Sellars, channeling the spirit of Protagoras, famously quipped that "in the dimension of describing and explaining the world, science is the measure of all things, of what is that it is, and of what is not that it is not" (1997, p. 83). Echoing this sentiment a decade later, Oxford chemistry professor Peter Atkins (2006) asserted that "Science is the only path to understanding" (p. 124). It is difficult to conceive of a more succinct description of the essential conceit of contemporary scientism. The only thing perhaps more difficult to conceive is precisely what scientific finding, or collection of such findings, it is that Atkins was relying on to establish the validity of his fundamentally philosophical assertion, or for that matter, to secure the truth of the metaphysical worldview upon which his claim rests. After all, if science itself is not the source of the claim, then how could we ever know it to be true—science being, as it is claimed, the *only* path to such understanding?

Still, despite the pesky persistence of such philosophical questions, a great many scientists, psychologists, and philosophers these days are content to make exactly these sorts of sweeping metaphysical and epistemological pronouncements about empirical science, seemingly untroubled by the fact that such pronouncements are fundamentally and inescapably nonempirical in nature. For champions of scientism, "only science is true and rational; everything else is mere belief or opinion, and it is science which tells us how the world really is" (Stratton, 2000, p. 2). Indeed, biologist Richard Lewontin (1997), in his review of Carl Sagan's *The Demon-Haunted World*, argued that it is long past time that people should "accept a social and intellectual apparatus, Science, as the only begetter of truth" (p. 28). It is just such a conceit that allows thinkers like Alexander Rosenberg (2011) to confidently assure us that

> the methods of science are the only reliable ways to secure knowledge of anything; that science's description of the world is correct in its fundamentals; and that when 'complete', what science tells us will not be surprisingly different from what it tells us today.
>
> (pp. 6–7; see also Atkins, 2011; Harris, 2010)[2]

And what exactly is it that science is telling us today and will continue to tell us tomorrow? Simply that "reality consists of nothing but a single all-embracing spatio-temporal system" (Armstrong, 1978, p. 261) in which there is no intentionality, no purpose or meaning or value. Everything that exists is physical or material in nature, relentlessly and mechanically governed by immutable and impersonal natural law.

It is important to note here, however, that when scholars like Sellars, Atkins, Rosenberg, and others employ the term 'science', they have a fairly narrow and rigidly specific meaning in mind. For such thinkers, science means—and can only legitimately mean—a particular method of empirical investigation that relies entirely on the quantification and sensory observation of physical entities and processes in order to provide naturalistic explanations of the world, explanations framed solely in terms of the material constituents and mechanical-deterministic relationships that necessarily give rise to such phenomena. Indeed, advocates of scientism reject, in principle, any view of science that would suggest that there might exist or could exist any phenomena beyond the scope of such naturalistic explanation. In other words, that which cannot be measured by empirical means and thereby be fully explained in naturalistic terms does not in reality exist at all. E.L. Thorndike (1926) famously articulated just such a metaphysical view when he asserted: "If anything exists, it exists in some amount" (p. 38). Further, advocates of scientism like Jerry Fodor (2002) assure us that such a view is "not just true but *obviously and certainly* true; it's something that nobody in the late twentieth century who has a claim to an adequate education and a minimum of common sense should doubt" (p. 30). How exactly the validity of these sorts of claims has been—or ever could be—established scientifically, however, is unfortunately never really made clear in the work of those who make them. Nonetheless, once such conceits are granted, we are confidently assured, the real promise of science can begin to be realized. It is, in the end, to science alone we must look for salvation, for the solution to all our problems and the answers to all our (answerable) questions. "Science has no boundaries," we are told, and "eventually it will answer all theoretical questions and provide solutions for all our practical problems" (Radnitzky, 1978, p. 1008). Capturing this utopic vision of scientism nicely, Jawaharlal Nehru, India's first prime minister, once famously prophesied: "The future belongs to science and to those who make friends with science" (Nehru, 1976, p. 806).

It should come as no surprise that the assured, forward-looking, and hope-filled affirmations of these advocates for scientific naturalism have struck some observers as (ironically) reflecting more of an overzealous religious faith than genuinely scientific or empirical humility (see, e.g., Bolger, 2012; Midgley, 2002; Principe, 2015; Stenmark, 2001). For example, philosopher John Searle (2004) has noted:

> There is a sense in which [scientism] is the religion of our time, at least among most of the professional experts in the fields of philosophy, psychology, cognitive science, and other disciplines that study the mind. Like more traditional religions, it is accepted without question and it provides the framework within which other questions can be posed, addressed, and answered.
>
> (p. 48)

More recently, Hutchinson (2011) has argued that "in so far as scientism is an overarching world-view, it is fair to regard it as essentially a religious position" (p. 3). Noting that advocates of scientism would likely bristle at such a depiction—likely countering that scientism ought not be considered religious because it entails no belief in the supernatural and does not require any rituals or ceremonies—Hutchinson points out there are in fact recognized religions that "don't involve a belief in God, and religions that don't require participation in ceremonies" (p. 3). While definitely not offering a traditional theistic worldview, the materialist naturalism in which scientism is grounded offers a clearly religious framework for answering "our existential questions: it can tell us why we are here, where we come from, and where we are going" (Stenmark, 2001, p. 14). And "since there are really no differences between science and scientific materialism, science can be, and *should* be, our religion" (Stenmark, 2001, p. 14).

Strangely, it seems to increasingly be the case that the healthy attitude of critical self-reflection and skepticism, long noted hallmarks of the scientific mind, have been largely abandoned by the zealous advocates of scientism, at least insofar as taking a careful look at their own philosophical and methodological presuppositions is concerned (see Reber in this volume). No longer recognizing any real need for penetrating or critical self-reflection about the possible limits of empiricist methodology, or the probable blind spots of reductive materialist naturalism, those who endorse the scientistic worldview have become profoundly self-assured proselytizers of a truth (naturalism) they believe to simply be no longer open to serious question or doubt. Whatever the case may be, however, it is seems clear that the central conceits of scientism are establishing a firm hold on the imaginations of not only professional scientists and philosophers, but the general public as well—although perhaps not as quickly as some defenders of scientism might like.

Evolutionary Psychology and Scientism

The discipline of psychology has long been a key player in the general effort to disseminate a scientistic view of the world, particularly in regards to the study, explanation, and meaning of human behavior (see Cowburn, 2013, pp. 61–74; Levin, 2001; Martin & Thompson, 1997). While it is certainly true that not all psychologists have endorsed the grand metaphysical and methodological claims of scientistic epistemology, or the materialist metaphysics that undergird that epistemology, the reductive spirit of scientism has nonetheless long defined modern psychological theory and practice for many in the discipline (see, e.g., Martin, Sugarman, & Thompson, 2003, especially chapter 2, "Reductionism in Psychology"). Indeed, as Alexander and Shelton (2014) have noted, "Materialism, determinism, and reductionism have been major features of professional psychology since its beginnings in the nineteenth century" (p. 240). Similarly, Gantt and Williams (2014) recently examined the "legacy of Newtonianism" in modern psychology, a legacy "principally characterized by explanations invoking mechanical, efficient causal determinism, and relying on the operation of universal laws manifest as forces, the effect of which can be described in mathematically precise ways" (p. 83).

Ironically, psychology's infatuation with the methods and epistemological aspirations of the natural sciences has managed to persist despite intense and sustained critique from a variety of credible sources both within and without the discipline—critique that began almost at the discipline's inception and that has continued to the present day. Indeed, as Martin, Sugarman, and Thompson (2003) note, "so strong has been the attachment of disciplinary psychology to its scientistic pretensions that, for the most part, psychologists have simply ignored such criticism" (p. 20). Why exactly the discipline has been able to ignore such criticism and proceed so confidently as though no real metaphysical or epistemological problems exist regarding the adoption of scientific methods for the study of human beings remains something of a mystery. Upon serious reflection, one is inclined to accept Charles Taylor's (1985) argument that the appeal of reductive naturalism in modern psychology arises out of ideological grounds more than anything else, that scientism's "epistemological weaknesses are more than made up for by its moral appeal" (p. 6).

Even a fairly superficial perusal of the way in which scientific method is treated in almost any introductory textbook on research methods in psychology is sufficient to demonstrate that a scientistic conception of the methods of scientific investigation is considered superior to all other possible approaches to obtaining reliable, genuine knowledge (see, e.g., treatments of methods of inquiry and explanation in Bordens & Abbott, 2013; Evans & Rooney, 2014; McBride, 2013; White & McBurney, 2013). For example, in their introduction to psychological research Goodwin and Goodwin (2012) claim that "The most reliable way to develop a belief . . . is through the method of science" (p. 9).[3] Likewise, McBride (2013) asserts, "Psychologists use the scientific method because it provides the best way to gain knowledge about behavior" (p. 13). Further, only reductive naturalistic (i.e., material, mechanical, and deterministic) explanations of human behavior are held to possess any real epistemological merit. Indeed, as Bechtel and Wright (2009) note, "mechanistic explanation provides [the] unifying framework that integrates a variety of explanatory projects in psychology" (p. 127).

Although there are many examples of scientistic thinking in contemporary psychology one could employ as a case study, in this chapter I will focus primarily on evolutionary psychology (EP), its theoretical assumptions, methodological commitments, and explanatory strategies. Like most scientistic projects in psychology, EP relies on very circumscribed conceptions of theory and method in its attempt to provide a thoroughgoing naturalistic account of all human behavior. Indeed, many evolutionary psychologists argue that the evolutionary perspective is nothing less than the "gold standard for a scientific explanation" (Pinker, 2005, p. xii), and as such "represents a true scientific revolution, a profound paradigm shift in the field of psychology" (Buss, 2005, p. xxiv). EP is, as Tooby and Cosmides (2005) have stated, "the long-forestalled scientific attempt to assemble out of the disjointed, fragmentary, and mutually contradictory human disciplines a single, logically integrated research framework for the psychological, social, and behavioral sciences" (p. 5). As such, EP promises to finally provide psychology with a "basic intellectual framework for understanding all psychological phenomena" that can serve as the "underlying meta-theory to guide all the behavioral sciences in the future" (Geher, 2006, p. 184). In the eyes of its adherents, unlike previous endeavors in psychological science, EP is able to achieve its lofty intellectual heights because EP researchers restrict themselves to employing only objective measures and reporting only empirical observations of natural phenomena so as to generate explanations that only invoke identifiable material elements, identifiable mechanical processes, and efficient causal relationships.

According to Crawford and Krebs (2008), there are at least six basic theoretical postulates that undergird the investigative and explanatory work of most contemporary evolutionary psychologists, irrespective of their areas of particular research focus. These basic postulates are:

1. Human behavior can (and should) be explained at both a proximate and ultimate level of analysis;
2. Domain specificity (i.e., adaptive problems) are solved through specific designated physical and behavioral structures or mental modules;
3. These mental mechanisms are innate; there is no genetic variation in them between people (except for those differences between the sexes related to differences in the ancestral problems they faced);
4. Human nature is explained best as the product of genes and environment;
5. The workings of most mental mechanisms are not available to consciousness;
6. There are differences between the current and ancestral environment that may have influenced the functioning or outcome of evolved mechanisms (see Crawford & Krebs, 2008, p. 13).

Each of these theoretical postulates, in turn, rests on an even more basic set of philosophical assumptions regarding the nature of reality, the source and character of its various operations, and the proper epistemological means (i.e., scientific empiricism) by which we might discover the particularities of those operations. At minimum, these deeper philosophical assumptions include commitments to reductive naturalism, material mechanism, and necessary determinism (see Cunningham, 2010; Gantt, 2017; Gantt & Melling, 2009; Gantt, Melling, & Reber, 2012; Menuge, 2004). Indeed, as Hoffman (2016) states in his *Philosophical Foundations of Evolutionary Psychology*, the materialist philosophy first articulated by the ancient Greeks, which holds that "physical sciences of the world can account for and explain all components of human behavior . . . provides the foundation from which evolutionary psychology developed" (p. 85). Ultimately, then, EP explanations of human behavior rely entirely on (1) the identification of certain basic material conditions and (2) the postulation of particular psychological mechanisms and processes presumed to arise from those material conditions, and which are, in turn, held to produce in efficient causal fashion all specific behavioral outcomes.

Unlike earlier sociobiological accounts of behavior, which also relied heavily on an evolutionary perspective, EP accounts do not seek to establish an essentially one-to-one connection between specific behaviors and particular genetic or biological conditions. Indeed, evolutionary psychologists often take great pains to deny critics who claim that EP entails the same sort of genetic reductionism that was so characteristic of sociobiology (see, e.g., Geher, 2006).

In contrast to sociobiology, EP maintains that between the biological reality of the gene and the social reality of human behavior there necessarily exist certain species-specific psychological mechanisms that must be invoked in order to secure a legitimately psychological explanation of behavior that is at the same time grounded in the biological context of evolutionary theory. Indeed, evolutionary psychologists like David Buss frequently argue that "all behavior owes its existence to underlying psychological mechanisms" and that the central task of evolutionary psychology is to "discover, describe, and explain the nature of those mechanisms" (Buss, 1995, p. 6). "Because all behavior depends on complex psychological mechanisms," Buss (1995) asserts, "and all psychological mechanisms, at some basic level of description, are the result of evolution by selection, then all psychological theories are implicitly evolutionary psychological theories" (p. 2). In short, for evolutionary psychologists, the explanation of the origin and nature of these "underlying psychological mechanisms" is found in "a set of principles which, at its core, simply asserts that the human nervous system and resultant behavior are ultimately products of organic evolutionary processes" (Geher, 2006, p. 184). Thus, the psychological mechanisms presumed to produce human behavior (including cognition and emotion) are themselves the product of the process of natural selection operating on biological organisms, both currently and (more importantly) in the distant past. In this fashion, evolutionary psychologists hypothesize a number of psychological constructs that can serve as both cause (the mechanism) and effect (the psychological trait) in order to maintain disciplinary focus on the human mind, and thereby avoid some of the conceptual pitfalls (e.g., overly simplistic genetic reductionism) that beset their sociobiological predecessors.

Buss (1995) and other evolutionary psychologists often portray their work as contributing to the ongoing and unparalleled success of science in "uncovering the mysteries of life" (p. 25) because it "provides the key to unlocking the mystery of where we came from, how we arrived at our current state, and the mechanisms of mind that define who we are" (p. 27). Just who exactly we are revealed to be in this perspective can be clearly seen in this description offered by Tooby and Cosmides (1992), where they claim that human beings are really just:

> self-reproducing chemical systems, multicellular heterotrophic mobile organisms (animals), appearing very late in the history of life as somewhat modified versions of earlier primate designs. Our developmental programs, as well as the physiological and psychological mechanisms

that they reliably construct, are the natural product of this evolutionary history. Human minds, human behavior, human artifacts, and human culture are all biological phenomena—aspects of the phenotypes of humans and their relationships with one another.

(pp. 20–21)

Somewhat more directly, but by no means any less reductively, Brooks (2002) confesses:

> I believe myself and my children all to be mere machines. Automatons at large in the universe. Every person I meet is also a machine—a big bag of skin full of biomolecules interacting according to describable and knowable rules.
>
> (p. 174)[4]

While such a view of human nature may strike many readers as dismayingly bleak and drab, it is a view that, evolutionary psychologists maintain, the objective evidence of their science requires that we accept. To refuse to face the facts of the evolutionary account, it is argued, is to abandon all pretense to modern scientific rationality and retreat back into the medieval shadowlands of prescientific superstitions and religious irrationalities (see, e.g., Atkins, 2011; Stenger, 2009). Indeed, for some there is a war to be fought here, a war "between rationalism and superstition" (Coyne, cited in Dawkins, 2006, p. 67), a war where the adherents of evolutionary scientism in psychology are arrayed in noble defense of rationality on one side, while any who have yet to see the intellectual light are consigned to the infidel forces of cultural and intellectual regression on the other.[5]

Perhaps this sort of forced choice would be more troubling, as well as more compelling, were it reflective of a legitimate problem rather than simply a false dichotomy arising out of overly narrow and philosophically naïve understandings of the nature and capacities of science—narrow and naïve understandings rooted in an unwarranted equation of science, per se, with the metaphysics of reductive naturalism. If science were in fact just as the scientistic advocates of EP so frequently depict it, then surely there would be reason for consternation regarding our more traditional conceptions of not only human nature, but also knowledge, reason, meaning, and truth (see, e.g., Gantt & Melling, 2009; Menuge, 2004; Nagel, 2012). Were it truly the case that the findings and theoretical postulations of evolutionary psychologists revealed the indisputable facts of nature and nature's laws as discovered through the relentlessly dispassionate application of unbiased and value-free empirical method, then perhaps there would be real reason to reject outright the philosophical, religious, and experiential claims of other traditions.

Unfortunately, at least for its advocates, the question of the empirical validity, as well as the philosophical coherence, of EP findings and theory is still very much alive and open for debate (see, e.g., Buller, 2006; Cunningham, 2010; Dupré, 2001; Gantt, 2017; Gantt & Melling, 2009; Gantt, Melling, & Reber, 2012; Nagel, 2012; Rose & Rose, 2000; Tallis, 2011).

Ultimately, before the scientistic aspirations of EP can be fully realized, its adherents must confront both the reality of the inherent limitations of the methods of science they embrace and the explanatory constraints of the reductive naturalistic metaphysic they assume. The noted historian of science Michael J. Crowe (2001) has shown that "Throughout much of history, one of the major positions in the methodology of science has been what is sometimes referred to as the 'save the phenomena' position" (p. 66). "The basic tenet of this position," he continues, "is that judgments of the value of a scientific theory should be made in terms of only two criteria: the ability of the theory to save (account for or predict) the phenomena and the theory's simplicity" (p. 66). In a similar spirit, as part of his Gifford Lectures in 1997, Rolston also noted: "We often forget how everyday experience can demand certain things of the sciences. Science must save the phenomena . . . [and if a given scientific theory or methodological approach cannot] . . . so much the worse for that theory" (1999, p. xv).

Maintaining an open methodological and philosophical attitude, one in which saving the phenomena is of paramount importance, is vital to the genuinely scientific study of human experience and behavior. Unfortunately, this sort of conceptual and methodological openness is something that adherents of scientism steadfastly resist. Sociologist Douglas Porpora (2006) has trenchantly argued:

> In any proper experience, the object of experience contributes something to the content of experience. The object, in other words, is part of what explains the content. Yet if objects of experience . . . are methodologically bracketed out of consideration, they are disallowed a priori from doing any explanatory work. The unavoidable implication is that there are no genuine experiences of anything so that the very category of experience dissolves.
>
> (pp. 58–59)

In other words, only by taking human experience seriously—that is, by treating the phenomena of human experience on their own terms as fundamentally meaningful expressions of human social and moral reality, rather than simply reducing them to methodological or conceptual categories that may be quite alien to them—can a genuinely fruitful psychological science emerge. In order to adequately understand the behavior of people, then, psychologists must first seek to sincerely and openly understand the experiential grounds of such behavior. "Minimally," Porpora (2006) argues, "that means not to rule out *tout court* what people say they are experiencing" (p. 59).

Unfortunately, denying outright the reality and meaning and intentional origins of human actions and experiences is precisely the sort of thing that EP does, and precisely so because of its fundamental commitment to the reductive naturalism of the scientistic worldview. "Only a theory that explained conscious events in terms of unconscious events," advocates of EP claim, "could explain consciousness at all" (Dennett, 1991, p. 454). The ultimate goal of the reductively naturalistic account of human action by evolutionary psychologists is "to take the beliefs, desires, preferences, choices, and so on that appear to make up our conscious, intelligent, psychological life and explain them in terms that are nonconscious, nonmental, and nonpsychological" (Goetz & Taliaferro, 2008, p. 16). Of course, in the process of such reductionism, all genuine meaning, value, and purpose disappear utterly from the world of human actions and relationships. However, the only justification for taking this reductive explanatory step in the first place seems to be because it is demanded by the metaphysical and methodological orthodoxies of modern scientism.

Clearly, then, the unfortunate result of evolutionary psychologists' having adopted the orthodoxies of contemporary scientism is that they are forced into a fundamental dilemma in which they must, as Belzen (1997) has noted, "either to be faithful to the demands of the life-world and not do justice to science, or to remain faithful to the requirements of science and, precisely because of that, fail to do justice to the life-world" (p. 8). Of course, the viability of the dilemma Belzen identifies depends entirely on the highly questionable presumption that a defining requirement of science *qua* science is a commitment to reductive naturalism. By restricting investigation solely to measureable physical entities and events—and, concomitantly, restricting explanation solely to physical, natural causes and hypothetical psychological mechanisms—EP inherently and inescapably hamstrings any genuine psychological inquiry into the nature and meaning of human experiences by virtue of the fact that so much of human experience is, by its very nature, reflective of what the French philosopher Jean-Luc Marion (2002a, 2002b) has termed "saturated phenomena."

Marion and Saturated Phenomena

Although seldom invoked in discussions of scientism in psychology, the work of the contemporary French philosopher Jean-Luc Marion has, I believe, considerable relevance to the critique of the project of scientism in the psychology generally and the case of EP specifically. Born on the outskirts of Paris in 1946, Marion studied at the University of Nanterre and the Sorbonne before doing graduate work in philosophy at the École Normale Supérieure in Paris, where he studied with key French thinkers of the 20th century such as Jacques Derrida, Louis Althusser, and Gilles Deleuze. Although much of his graduate work (and subsequent writing) was focused on the early thinking of Descartes, Marion also expressed a deep fascination with theological questions and an earnest concern with the nature and limits of phenomenological method, especially as articulated in the works of Edmund Husserl and Martin Heidegger (see Horner, 2005). A prolific writer, Marion's work has consistently addressed a number of important and highly controversial subjects in postmodern thought, traditional phenomenological and hermeneutic philosophy, and contemporary theology. Of particular interest to the analysis here, however, is what many take to be his most significant contribution to current intellectual discourse: the concept of the "saturated phenomenon" (Marion, 1996). Put simply, this is the notion that "there are phenomena of such overwhelming givenness or overflowing fulfillment that the intentional acts aimed at these phenomena are overrun, flooded—or saturated" (Caputo, 2007, p. 164).

According to Marion (2002b), in his book *Being Given: Toward a Phenomenology of Givenness*, human experience reveals varying degrees of phenomenality that range all the way from relatively impoverished phenomena at one pole—such as those found in mathematics and formal logic, where "what shows itself in and from itself does not need much more than its concept alone . . . to give itself" (p. 222)—to saturated phenomena at the other. Saturated phenomena, according to Marion, are those phenomena that intrinsically overflow and escape whatever conceptual boundaries we might seek to put them in. They are those phenomena that exhibit such overflowing "givenness" and flooding surplus in their unfolding that our experience of them is of overwhelming excess (i.e., saturation). As such, "a saturated phenomenon is one that cannot be wholly contained within concepts that can be grasped by our understanding" because in its very givenness, the very experience of the phenomenon as what it is, "there is always an excess left over, which is beyond conceptualization" (Mackinlay, 2010, p. 1). Saturated phenomena are thus intrinsically excessive, irruptive, and overflowing, and thus resist all attempts at reduction or mechanical and efficient causal explanation. In other words, saturated phenomena are those phenomena that are inherently too meaningful to be adequately or exhaustively captured by the tools and abstract categories of traditional scientific or rational thought. There is thus always 'something more' to such phenomena, an excess that constitutes the phenomena as what they are, but that cannot be fully articulated or expressed in any one language or medium—or, even, in some combination of all such languages and media.

For Marion, religious experiences are prime examples of saturated phenomena, although they are by no means the only such examples. Marion is clear that by identifying a given experience as being saturated, it does not mean that such experience is fundamentally mystical (at least, in the dualistic sense in which that term is traditionally understood). Saturated phenomena, religious or otherwise, are not best understood as simply the products of some force or entity that mysteriously and inexplicably intrudes into our natural world from the hidden recesses of some inaccessible other world that exists beyond our understanding. Rather, Marion suggests that religious experiences, like all saturated phenomena, are part and parcel of the world of meaningful human experience and, therefore, both natural (in a fully nonreductive sense) AND excessive. While by its very nature meaningful human experience exceeds the capacities of reductive methods of study and explanation, this does not imply that such experience is necessarily mysterious, inaccessibly subjective, or supernatural in some otherworldly sense.

Thus human experiences also exceed such constraining modes of understanding in the same sense that historical events like the Battle of Waterloo or the Holocaust constitute genuinely saturated phenomena, because they are not the sorts of things that can ever be adequately measured or fully reduced to the status of mere physical events produced solely by the interplay of material entities and mechanical forces. And in the same way that we would not claim that the Battle of Waterloo or the tragedy of the Holocaust must therefore be fundamentally unintelligible or supernatural phenomena—and, as such, off-limits to rigorous scientific investigation—genuinely meaningful human experiences are not unworthy of careful study just because they inherently embody more meaning than any particular investigatory approach (or collection of investigatory approaches) can fully capture or articulate.

Indeed, it may well be that the assumption that any phenomena not readily accessible to or explicable in straightforwardly naturalistic terms must therefore be supernatural and thus unintelligible, epistemologically inaccessible, and ultimately scientifically irrelevant is only a viable assumption if one grants epistemological priority to reductive naturalism in the first place. If, however, we can recognize some of the ways in which reductive naturalism might force our research focus to shift from the phenomena of actual interest (i.e., human experience as actually lived) and towards something else entirely (e.g., measureable behaviors, scans of brain activity, or quantified self-reports of abstract beliefs), then perhaps we can also recognize that it might be a mistake to dualistically partition the world of psychologically interesting phenomena into natural and supernatural or objective and subjective in the first place. By taking the reality and epistemological accessibility—although not explanatory exhaustibility—of saturated phenomena seriously, in the way that Marion suggests, perhaps it will finally be possible for psychologists to offer sensitive and respectful descriptions of actual human experience on its own terms. In order for such a development to begin to take place, however, the discipline must reject the flawed conceptual model—so clearly manifest in evolutionary psychology—of a scientistic enterprise committed to an overly narrow conception of the nature of science, scientific method, and human being.

Notes

1 As cited in Michael D. Aeschliman, *The Restitution of Man: C. S. Lewis and the Case Against Scientism*, p. 30.
2 It is, perhaps, fortunate that Rosenberg did not pen those words in 1904, just prior to Einstein's paradigm-shattering publications on relativity so thoroughly overturning the Newtonian worldview that constituted the scientific description of the world that held dominant sway during the previous two centuries.
3 Again, as with the Atkins quote cited earlier, one wonders how exactly scientific method was employed (in any non-question-begging way) to develop the belief that the most reliable way to develop a belief is through the method of science.
4 One wonders what a psychiatrist might make of such beliefs had they been offered up by an ordinary person who happened to wander in off the street, rather than by a noted and widely respected research scientist and author like Brooks.
5 There is, perhaps, some evidence for how serious this distinction between those who are intellectually enlightened on the one hand, and those benighted souls who have yet to see the light on the other, in the suggestion made by Richard Dawkins, Daniel Dennett, and others that advocates of a thoroughgoing neo-Darwinian worldview should proudly begin calling themselves "Brights."

References

Aeschliman, M. D. (1998). *The restitution of man: C. S. Lewis and the case against scientism*. Grand Rapids, MI: Wm. B. Eerdmans.
Alexander, B. K., & Shelton, C. P. (2014). *A history of psychology in Western civilization*. Cambridge: Cambridge University Press.
Armstrong, D. (1978). Naturalism, materialism, and first philosophy. *Philosophia, 8*, 261–276.
Atkins, P. (2006). Atheism and science. In P. Clayton & Z. Simpson (Eds.), *The Oxford handbook of religion and science* (pp. 124–136). Oxford: Oxford University Press.
Atkins, P. (2011). *On being: A scientist's exploration of the great questions of existence*. Oxford: Oxford University Press.
Bechtel, W., & Wright, C. D. (2009). What is psychological explanation? In J. Symons & P. Calvo (Eds.), *The Routledge companion to philosophy of psychology* (pp. 113–130). London: Routledge.
Belzen, J. A. (1997). The varieties of psychology of religion: By way of introduction. In J. A. Belzen (Ed.), *Hermeneutic approaches in psychology of religion* (pp. 7–10). Atlanta, GA: Rodolpi.

Bolger, R. K. (2012). *Kneeling at the altar of science: The mistaken path of contemporary religious scientism*. Eugene, OR: Wipf and Stock.

Bordens, K. S., & Abbott, B. B. (2013). *Research design and methods: A process approach* (6th ed.). Boston, MA: McGraw-Hill.

Brooks, R. (2002). *Flesh and machines: How robots will change us*. New York: Pantheon Books.

Buller, D. J. (2006). *Adapting minds: Evolutionary psychology and the persistent quest for human nature*. Cambridge, MA: MIT Press.

Buss, D. M. (1995). Evolutionary psychology: A new paradigm for psychological science. *Psychological Inquiry, 6*(1), 1–30.

Buss, D. M. (Ed.). (2005). Introduction: The emergence of evolutionary psychology. In D. M. Buss (Ed.), *The handbook of evolutionary psychology* (pp. xxiii–xxv). Hoboken, NJ: John Wiley and Sons.

Caputo, J. D. (2007). The erotic phenomenon by Jean-Luc Marion (Book Review). *Ethics, 118*(1), 164–168.

Cowburn, J. S. (2013). *Scientism: A word we need*. Eugene, OR: Wipf and Stock.

Crawford, C., & Krebs, D. (Eds.). (2008). *Foundations of evolutionary psychology*. New York: Lawrence Erlbaum Associates.

Crowe, M. J. (2001). *Theories of the world from antiquity to the Copernican revolution* (2nd ed., revised). Mineola, NY: Dover.

Cunningham, C. (2010). *Darwin's pious idea: Why the ultra-Darwinists and creationists both get it wrong*. Grand Rapids, MI: Wm. B. Eerdmans.

Dawkins, R. (2006). *The god delusion*. Boston, MA: Houghton Mifflin.

Dennett, D. (1991). *Consciousness explained*. Boston, MA: Little, Brown.

Dupré, J. (2001). *Human nature and the limits of science*. Oxford: Clarendon Press.

Evans, A. N., & Rooney, B. J. (2014). *Methods in psychological research* (3rd ed.). Thousand Oaks, CA: Sage.

Fodor, J. (2002). Is science biologically possible? In J. Beilby (Ed.), *Naturalism defeated? Essays on Plantinga's evolutionary argument against naturalism*. Ithaca, NY: Cornell University Press.

Gantt, E. E. (2017). Morality, red in tooth and claw: How evolutionary psychology renders morality meaningless. In E. E. Gantt (Ed.), *Taking sides: Clashing views on psychological issues* (20th ed., pp. 21–26). Dubuque, IA: McGraw-Hill.

Gantt, E. E., & Melling, B. S. (2009). Evolutionary psychology ain't evil, it's just not any good. In B. D. Slife (Ed.), *Taking sides: Clashing views on psychological issues* (Vol. 16, pp. 122–130). Dubuque, IA: McGraw-Hill.

Gantt, E. E., Melling, B. S., & Reber, J. S. (2012). Mechanisms or metaphors: The emptiness of evolutionary psychological explanations. *Theory and Psychology, 22*(6), 823–841.

Gantt, E. E., & Williams, R. N. (2014). Psychology and the legacy of Newtonianism: Motivation, intentionality, and the ontological gap. *Journal of Theoretical and Philosophical Psychology, 34*(2), 83–100.

Geher, G. (2006). Evolutionary psychology is not evil! (. . . and here's why . . .). *Psychological Topics, 15*(2), 181–202.

Goetz, S., & Taliaferro, C. (2008). *Naturalism*. Grand Rapids, MI: Wm. B. Eerdmans.

66   *Edwin E. Gantt*

Goodwin, C. J., & Goodwin, K. A. (2012). *Research in psychology: Methods and design* (7th ed.). Hoboken, NJ: John Wiley and Sons.
Harris, S. (2010). *The moral landscape: How science can determine human values.* New York: Free Press.
Hoffman, A. J. (2016). *Philosophical foundations of evolutionary psychology.* Lanham, MD: Lexington Books.
Horner, R. (2005). *Jean-Luc Marion: A theo-logical introduction.* Farnham: Ashgate.
Hutchinson, I. H. (2011). *Monopolizing knowledge: A scientist refutes religion-denying, reason-destroying scientism.* Belmont, MA: Fias.
Levin, Y. (2001). *The tyranny of reason: The origins and consequences of the social scientific outlook.* Lanham, MD: University Press of America.
Lewontin, R. C. (1997, January 9). Billions and billions of demons. *New York Review of Books.*
Mackinlay, S. (2010). *Interpreting excess: Jean-Luc Marion, saturated phenomena, and hermeneutics.* New York: Fordham University Press.
Marion, J-L. (1996). The saturated phenomenon. *Philosophy Today, 40*(1), 103–124.
Marion, J-L. (2002a). *In excess: Studies in saturated phenomena* (R. Horner & V. Berrand, Trans.). New York: Fordham University Press.
Marion, J-L. (2002b). *Being given: Toward a phenomenology of givenness* (J. L. Kosky, Trans.). Stanford, CA: Stanford University Press.
Martin, J., Sugarman, J., & Thompson, J. (2003). *Psychology and the question of agency.* Albany: State University of New York Press.
Martin, J., & Thompson, J. (1997). Between scientism and relativism: Phenomenology, hermeneutics, and the new realism in psychology. *Theory and Psychology, 7*(5), 629–652.
McBride, D. M. (2013). *The process of research in psychology* (2nd ed.). Thousand Oaks, CA: Sage.
Menuge, A. (2004). *Agents under fire: Materialism and the rationality of science.* Oxford: Rowman & Littlefield.
Midgley, M. (2002). *Evolution as religion* (2nd ed.). New York: Routledge.
Nagel, T. (2012). *Mind and cosmos: Why the materialist Neo-Darwinian conception of nature is almost certainly false.* Oxford: Oxford University Press.
Nehru, J. (1976). *Selected works of Jawaharlal Nehru* (Vol. 8). New Delhi: Orient Longman.
Pinker, S. (2005). Foreword. In D. Buss (Ed.), *Handbook of evolutionary psychology* (pp. xi–xvi). Hoboken, NJ: John Wiley and Sons.
Porpora, D. V. (2006). Methodological atheism, methodological agnosticism, and religious experience. *Journal for the Theory of Social Behavior, 36*(1), 57–75.
Principe, L. M. (2015). Scientism and the religion of science. In R. N. Williams & D. N. Robinson (Eds.), *Scientism: The new orthodoxy* (pp. 41–62). New York: Bloomsbury Academic.
Radnitzky, G. (1978). The boundaries of science and technology. In *The search for absolute values in a changing world* (Vol. 2, pp. 1007–1012). New York: International Cultural Foundations Press.
Rolston, H. (1999). *Genes, genesis, and god: Values and their origins in natural and human history.* Cambridge: Cambridge University Press.

Rose, H., & Rose, S. (Eds.). (2000). *Alas, poor Darwin: Arguments against evolutionary psychology*. New York: Random House.

Rosenberg, A. (2011). *The atheist's guide to reality: Enjoying life without illusions*. New York: W. W. Norton.

Searle, J. (2004). *Mind: A brief introduction*. Oxford: Oxford University Press.

Sellars, W. (1997). *Empiricism and the philosophy of mind*. Cambridge, MA: Harvard University Press.

Stenger, V. J. (2009). *The new atheism: Taking a stand for science and reason*. Amherst, NY: Prometheus Books.

Stenmark, M. (2001). *Scientism: Science, ethics, and religion*. London: Routledge.

Stratton, S. B. (2000). *Coherence, consonance, and conversation: The quest of theology, philosophy, and natural science for a unified world-view*. Lanham, MD: University Press of America.

Tallis, R. (2011). *Aping mankind: Neuromania, Darwinitis, and the misrepresentation of humanity*. Durham, UK: Acumen.

Taylor, C. (1985). *Human agency and language: Philosophical papers* (Vol. 1). Cambridge: Cambridge University Press.

Thorndike, E. L. (1926). *The measurement of intelligence*. New York: Teacher's College, Columbia University Press.

Tooby, J., & Cosmides, L. (1992). The psychological foundations of culture. In J. H. Barkow, L. Cosmides, & J. Tooby (Eds.), *The adapted mind: Evolutionary psychology and the generation of culture* (pp. 19–136). New York: Oxford University Press.

Tooby, J., & Cosmides, L. (2005). Conceptual foundations of evolutionary psychology. In D. Buss (Ed.), *The handbook of evolutionary psychology* (pp. 5–67). Hoboken, NJ: John Wiley and Sons.

White, T. L., & McBurney, D. H. (2013). *Research methods* (9th ed.). Belmont, CA: Wadsworth.

6 Psychotherapy and Scientism

Brent D. Slife, Eric A. Ghelfi, and
Sheilagh T. Fox

At this point in this volume, scientism has been conceptualized and its tenets and products have been critiqued. Our first question in this chapter is relatively straightforward: Does this conceptualization and critique apply to the psychotherapy literature? As we will attempt to explain, the answer is affirmative, at least for the vast majority of this research. We also realize, however, that this answer raises another intriguing question: If scientism really is so dominant and so problematic, why is there not some general uprising of dissatisfaction among those attempting to use it in the field? As it happens, there *is* a high degree of dissatisfaction and, perhaps more surprisingly, this dissatisfaction is relatively well known among psychotherapists and researchers of psychotherapy. Scientism just isn't typically viewed as one of the sources of this dissatisfaction.[1]

If, however, scientism is an important source of this dissatisfaction, why didn't the field of psychotherapy identify it long ago, and why hasn't it altered course in light of this dissatisfaction? Part of the answer, as we show, is the endemic nature of scientism. Scientism is so ingrained and so embedded in the field of psychotherapy that those who are dissatisfied do not see how it can be constructively addressed. Most researchers and practitioners of psychotherapy perceive no alternative; the dissatisfied have no place to go. We then conclude the chapter by offering a brief sketch of an alternative to the scientism of this literature—methodological pluralism. This pluralism proffers a question-driven rather than a method-driven approach, which we believe is more in keeping with authentic science.

Clarifying Scientism

We first need to clarify scientism generally and then elaborate it for the purposes of the psychotherapy literature. To do so, it is important to understand that the historical formulation of any method of investigation requires the formulator to make certain preinvestigatory assumptions, whether explicit or implicit, about the nature of the world (its ontology) in order to know what features of method (its epistemology) would be the most successful in that world. Subsequent researchers may become less aware of these assumptions as the methods are used over time, but this does not mean the assumptions are no longer involved. Indeed, any time a researcher deploys the methods 'correctly', such as using certain investigation procedures or strategies, the justifications and even guidelines for using these features—their assumptions— are implicit. Scientism, then, is the affirmation of a *particular* set of these method assumptions to the *exclusion* of other method assumptions. This conscious or unconscious narrowing to an exclusive set of method assumptions is what distinguishes scientism from science. As the noted historian of science Feyerabend (1995) put it: "science is not one thing; it is many; it is not closed, but open to new approaches" (p. 809).

In the case of the psychotherapy literature, we will attempt to describe how the set of epistemological assumptions is the common notion of empiricism: knowledge comes from sensory experience, especially that of visual observation (Slife & Williams, 1995; Slife & Slife, 2014). The particular ontology in this literature is the familiar conception of naturalism: the natural world is generally governed by natural laws or generalities of varying sorts, such as principles and mechanisms (Kazdin, 2002, 2007). This combination of empiricism and naturalism is sometimes known as logical positivism or neo-positivism (Aragona, 2013; Barker, Pistrang, & Elliot, 2002), which has its own configuration of assumptions from this epistemology and ontology for psychotherapy research. We outline two general categories of these method assumptions here—lawfulness and dualism—that have spawned particular features or procedures for psychotherapy research, which we also describe.

Lawfulness

The naturalism of neopositivism assumes that methods should be designed to detect natural laws or regularities (Barker, Pistrang, & Elliot, 2002; Deacon, 2013; Rieken & Gelo, 2015). To accomplish this task, three manifestations or features of method are typically considered vital: generalization, comparability, and causality. Perhaps the most obvious of these features is the significance of generalization and replication. Without this feature, the regularity of natural laws or principles could not be discovered. As a second method feature within the category of lawfulness, natural laws and principles are best detected when the varied phenomena of science are rendered comparable. Comparability allows seemingly different phenomena to be examined for possible similarities of pattern, potentially indicating lawful principles or generalities of psychology. Representing everything in numbers or quantities is an important example of this method feature because numbers are singularly virtuous in finding patterns across differing research topics and situations. However, other characteristics of methods, such as standardization (e.g., manualization), may also facilitate comparison through minimizing differences and maximizing similarities among groups. As a third feature of method, laws that govern our reality are typically considered causal in nature, so experimental methods should be employed, as often as possible, that identify these causal laws.

Dualism

As a second major assumption of neopositivist methods, the term 'dualism' does not mean the familiar (and derided) Cartesian notion of mind/body. It is, instead, a related characteristic of Cartesian philosophy—the separability of the subjective from the objective—with the objective viewed as the real or truthful. Three method features are frequently manifested in attempting to accomplish this separation: subjectivity avoidance, objectivity as observability, and the translation of the subjective into the objective. First, researchers should be required to separate their biases and mere opinions—their subjectivity—from the objectivity of the real world. This feature is, of course, the familiar notion that subjectivity (bias, values) distorts investigation and should be reduced as much as possible to discern the true and objective world. As a second method feature of this form of dualism, the empiricism of neopositivism often leads researchers to presume that the objective realm of the world is best found through systematic observation. Because empiricism assumes that the sensory experience of vision is the most important pathway to knowledge, visual observation is considered pivotal. Indeed, observation is so pivotal in separating the objective from the subjective that it frequently entails use of the third feature of method: operationalization. This feature basically attempts to translate any phenomena or topics of interest that are not inherently observable into aspects or manifestations that are observable and thus ultimately objective.

In sum, the method assumptions of lawfulness and dualism frequently lead to six method features. The method assumption of lawfulness tends to spawn the method features of generalization, comparability, and causality, while the method assumption of dualism tends to manifest the method features of subjectivity avoidance, objectivity as observability, and the operationalization of the subjective into the objective.

Scientism in Psychotherapy Research

But do therapy researchers actually conduct their studies with these method features? We believe that even a cursory examination of therapy research bears this out, as do existing reviews in this regard (Clegg, 2016; Slife, Reber, & Faulconer, 2012; Slife & Williams, 1995; Slife, Wright, & Yanchar, 2016). However, therapy researchers rarely provide the most basic rationale for their method decisions in their articles. Controversial method decisions are, of course, discussed and defended, but an indicator of the pervasiveness and acceptance of the method features described earlier is that they are rarely discussed or defended; they are simply used. For these features, therapy researchers routinely refer and defer to psychological method texts, which we include here, along with examples of the psychotherapy literature, to illustrate scientism in use.

Lawfulness

As one of the preeminent methodologists of psychotherapy, Alan Kazdin (2002), explains: "Broadly conceived, methodology encompasses the procedures and practices of conducting and designing research so that lawful relations can be identified" (p. 12). Or consider Rieken and Gelo (2015): Therapy researchers "assume that the bewildering diversity of natural phenomena hides simple, eternal laws" (p. 70). In this sense, then, there is little doubt about the value ascribed to generalization. As Ray (2006), for example, puts it: "It must be possible for different people in different places and at different times using a similar method to produce the same results" (p. 7). Even the recent 'replication crisis'—that it *is* a crisis—is evidence of the importance of lawful phenomena in psychotherapy research (e.g., Christopherson, 2016; Open Science Collaboration, 2015; Russell, 2013).

We use the term 'lawful phenomena' here because the term 'law' is rarely used in the psychotherapy literature. Rather, the approximation of such laws is commonly sought, whether in the form of a psychological mechanism, principle, or merely the probability of a result pattern generalizing, as in this quote: "Most research has been done within the nomothetic tradition, which emphasizes pooling people together to look for commonalities, rather than the idiographic tradition, which emphasizes individual uniqueness" (Barker, Pistrang, & Elliot, 2002, p. 27). And because such lawful phenomena are frequently understood as causal laws, the seeking and finding of causal or deterministic relations are considered one of the best approximations of these laws: "Mainstream psychotherapy science has long adopted empiricism, reductionism, and determinism. . . . the cornerstone of contemporary psychotherapy research is to provide empirical evidence to the efficacy and mechanisms of actions of psychotherapeutic interventions" (Rieken & Gelo, 2015, p. 70).

The psychotherapy literature is also pervaded with features of method that accentuate nomothetic comparison across contexts to find these causal laws, such as randomization, quantification, and manualization (Rieken & Gelo, 2015; Shean, 2013; Weisz, Krumholz, Santucci, Thomassin, & Ng, 2015). This notion of comparability is epitomized by the method of randomized controlled trials (RCTs), as in this quote: "In the context of the increasing popularity of the biomedical model and pharmacological treatments in the 1970s, the NIMH [National Institute of Mental Health] designated the RCT as the standard method of evaluating psychotherapy and drug treatments" (Deacon, 2013, p. 853, brackets added). Even when difficulties with these approaches to comparison are acknowledged, their ascendancy is nevertheless affirmed. Consider Lilienfeld, Ritschel, Lynn, Cautin, and Latzman (2013) on quantification: "There may well be some truth to the proposition that certain changes in psychotherapy are difficult to measure, at least given presently available instruments. Yet as the great E. L. Thorndike (1940) observed, 'If something exists, then it exists in some quantity. If it exists in some quantity, then it can be measured' (p. 19)" (p. 893). Or consider Lilienfeld et al. (2013) on the issue of manualization: "Although psychotherapy training manuals are by no means required for EBP [evidence-based practice], they are one frequent means of maximizing the chances that practitioners engage in practices that are supported by controlled research" (p. 894).

Dualism

As described in the earlier section on "Clarifying Scientism," dualism is the neopositivist method assumption that the objective (real) world can and should be separated from the subjectivity of the researcher. This assumption has spurred, in turn, at least three features of method in psychotherapy research: subjectivity avoidance, objectivity as observability, and the operationalization of the subjective into the objective.

Regarding the first of these, Barker, Pistrang, and Elliot (2002) are quite clear: "The fundamental reason for the development of rigorous research methods is to attempt to minimize biases in drawing conclusions from evidence" (p. 9). Schweigert (2006) is also straightforward: "Scientists look for independent evidence of their claim: objective evidence that does not depend on the scientist's theory or personal viewpoint" (p. 2). Indeed, any indication of subjective biases in the data is a sure sign of problems with the researcher's objectivity, because the objective world is itself presumed to be free of subjectivity, and thus value-free. Schweigert (2006) again clarifies: "This approach is adopted so that the results of the research will be meaningful, unambiguous, and uncontaminated by the biases of either the participants or the researcher" (p. 2). Even the purpose of measurement is bias minimization: "The key benefit [of measurement] is objectivity, which minimizes subjective judgment and allows theories to be tested" (Coaley, 2009, p. 4).

The primary, if not exclusive, research path to this value-free, objective world of psychotherapy reality is thought to be through observation. As Stiles (2009) writes, "Researchers creatively modify their theories by (abductively) adding to them or altering them so that they correspond to accumulating observations" (p. 1). Objective observations, in this sense, are the correctives to our subjective theories. However, not all topics of interest are equally observable, in which case researchers must translate the unobservable into the observable. In other words, psychological researchers "must operationalize" (Furlong, Lovelace, & Lovelace, 2000, p. 63; Krathwohl, 2009, p. 141), and rigorous studies "need" or "require" operationalization (Borg & Gall, 1989, p. 65; Krathwohl, 2009, p. 140) because an operational definition "gives meaning to a variable" (Kerlinger & Lee, 2000, p. 43; see also Privitera, 2014, p. 89).

Openness to Alternatives

Recent APA statements concerning evidence-based practices (EBP) have appeared to express greater openness to methods that do not embody these method features, such as some qualitative methods (American Psychological Association, 2006). However, the neopositivist methods that include the features described earlier are nearly always favored. Wendt and Slife (2007) note the APA Task Force

> fails to understand and value qualitative research as a different philosophy of science. A clear signal that the Task Force misunderstands and misrepresents qualitative research is its use of the word 'subjective' in describing the purpose of qualitative research only. In the midst of a discipline that champions 'objective' inquiry, relegating qualitative methods to the 'subjective' is a second-class citizenship, at best.
>
> (p. 614)

As a case in point, consider how Lilienfeld et al. (2013) values RCTs, which embody all of the method features: "It is indeed the case that all else being equal, RCTs occupy a higher stratum in the hierarchy than do other sources of evidence" (p. 893).[2]

This 'hierarchy' or favoritism toward neopositivist methods is most frequently manifested as a kind of faith in science for all things psychological. In this regard, consider Barak (1995) who exemplifies those who deny that some processes of therapeutic interest are inaccessible to these method features: the "message that there must be factors operating through these processes which are above and beyond what (existing or still to be developed) scientific methods ought and should be able to explore is

74 Brent D. Slife et al.

unacceptable" (p. 309). Few therapy researchers would advocate the use of these methods for advancing knowledge in the humanities, but most would pledge full faith in them when psychologists run into humanities-oriented phenomena in client care, such as meaning, spirituality, or morality. Consider Barak (1995) again:

> None of us . . . would give up the prolonged scientific struggles to reach full understanding and valid predictions of earthquakes. In principle, the understanding of human character and behaviour is no different. I believe that it is only a question of much time, effort, *faith*, and commitment.
>
> (p. 312, emphasis added)

It may go without saying that these kinds of faith statements are not themselves empirical. There can be no empirical evidence supporting this statement, because it would be a "boot-strap problem," a method investigating itself.[3]

Rieken and Gelo (2015) aptly sum up the favored method features of psychotherapy researchers when referring to all the characteristics of scientism we have described:

> Mechanization is evident in mainstream psychotherapy research and in the prescriptions of its quantitative methodology . . .: experimental designs should be ideally used to test models of antecedent causality through the control of confounding variables and the exclusion of possible alternative explanations for the observed behaviors; big samples should be employed in order to allow time- and context-free generalizations of the results; standardized measurement by means of questionnaires and/or rating scales should be used for data collection, with the consequence of the richness of the patient's subjective experience being pushed into the background in favor of reliable measures of what is supposed to change; and statistics should be employed to describe and analyze relationships among the investigated constructs, so that the general laws governing the observed behaviors may be adequately tested.
>
> (p. 74)

Practitioner Dissatisfaction

One might assume that the pervasiveness of these method features, as summarized by Rieken and Gelo (2015), is an indication of their overwhelming acceptance and even popularity. However, this assumption would overlook an important element of dissatisfaction with this research. Indeed, the very people whom therapy investigations are most intended to serve are the least satisfied with it: psychotherapists. The therapy literature is unequivocal about "the troubled relationship between researchers and therapists," which has "been well documented in the literature" (Elliott & Morrow-Bradley, 1994, p. 124). Consider, for example, how Gyani, Shafran, Myles, and Rose (2014) sum up this literature: "The fact that, generally, clinicians prefer to rely on clinical experience rather than research to inform treatment decisions replicates previous studies" (p. 208; see also Beutler, Williams, & Wakefield, 1993; Beutler, Williams, Wakefield, & Entwistle, 1995; Morrow-Bradley & Elliott, 1986; Stewart & Chambless, 2007). Or consider the first-person experiences of Edelson (1994):

> I wish I could reply . . . by pointing to all the times I have turned to psychotherapy research for answers to the questions I ask myself as I do psychotherapy. To my chagrin, I can point to no instance, not one, where I have done so. I do not believe that, among psychotherapists, I am an exception.
>
> (p. 65)

Clearly, if therapy practitioners rarely depend on therapy research, therapy investigators may not be appropriately serving the stakeholders of this research. The next question, of course, is "why?" Why are therapy practitioners so dissatisfied with this research that they do not use it, especially when it is expressly intended for their benefit? In answering this question, it is not uncommon for commentators, such as Barker, Pistrang, and Elliot (2002), to note the positivist philosophy that typically underlies this research: "The positivist paradigm . . ., under which much research is conducted, is seen [by practicing psychologists] as being reductive and simplistic" (p. 27). Such commentators rarely point to scientism *per se*, but they do describe the features of positivist methods that are so troublesome for psychotherapists. Our limited space prevents a thorough review here, but consider this sampling of dissatisfaction statements in relation to the two categories of method assumptions, lawfulness and dualism, along with the six method features that we described as manifestations of these assumptions.

Lawfulness

Consider first the analysis of Barker, Pistrang, and Elliot (2002): "There is a tension between the scientific stance, which looks for generalities and lawfulness, and the clinical stance, which stresses human individuality" (p. 38). Therapists somehow experience a disconnect between the search for lawful generalities across many research situations and the nature of therapy within an individual situation. Perhaps the most prominent expression of this disconnect for dissatisfied therapists is the *complexity* of therapy: "Claims [of therapy researchers] are in my view misleading and simplistic, and it is this 'outcome research' I have a problem with. It does justice neither to the complexity of people's psychology nor to the intricacies of psychotherapy" (Marzillier, 2004, p. 392). Apparently, the method features that help to make dissimilar therapy phenomena comparable and thus generalizable tend to obscure their complexity:

> the delivery of a fixed number of psychotherapy sessions in close adherence with a step-by-step manual, while useful in operationally defining independent variables in an RCT, bears little resemblance to routine clinical practice and is perceived by many clinicians as unduly restrictive.
>
> (Deacon, 2013, p. 854)

We should acknowledge here that the metaphysic of positivism does not deny the complexity of nature (or social phenomena). It merely assumes that there are laws 'behind' this complexity, and thus the generalizations produced by research should be relevant and ultimately helpful. However, as the complaints of practicing therapists tend to illustrate, the path between the complicated particulars of practice and the simple generalities of research is not easily traversed. Consider Edelson (1994) again in this regard:

> I wonder if the conclusions derived from clinical research are applicable in the 'contaminated' situation in which I do psychotherapy, where these conclusions are, at best, approximately true because many things are going on at once and some causes may cancel the influence of others.
>
> (p. 64, emphasis added)

Indeed, one could wonder if the two types of phenomena—the particulars of practice and the generalities of research—are qualitatively different in many ways:

> The important point here is that which particulars present themselves on any occasion depends on a thousand contingencies that enter into that occasion, and perhaps no other occasion. The occurrence of such ad hoc contingent particulars cannot be predicted from general laws.
>
> (Edelson, 1994, pp. 65–66)

If Edelson is right, and "contingent particulars cannot be predicted from general laws," then therapy researchers are routinely gathering knowledge that therapists cannot use. At the very least, the relationship between the generalities of research and the particulars of therapy is not as straightforward as neopositivists would lead us to believe. Unfortunately, the field of psychotherapy rarely discusses the philosophical issues inherent in this relationship. Edelson's (1994) reference to predictability also points to a similar problem that is rarely examined or discussed, the issue of causality, which is another method feature of lawfulness:

> Psychotherapists do not pin their hopes on prediction. When they are interested in causal explanation at all, they are interested not only in what causes what but in how many numbers of causes combine to bring about an effect by specific means or mechanisms.
>
> (p. 69)

The upshot here is that many of the dissatisfactions of therapists such as Edelson ultimately find their root in the philosophies of positivism that direct the researcher to formulate their methods to search for law-like phenomena.

Dualism

The second method assumption of the scientism of psychotherapy research is that of dualism, the philosophical assumption that the objective and subjective realms can and should be separated to distill the objective world, which is considered the knowledge base of therapeutic reality. Recall that we singled out three main method features that were manifestations of this dualist assumption: the need to avoid subjectivity (e.g., personal biases, values, opinions) in research; the emphasis on the observable to get to the objective psychological world; and the mandate to operationalize those psychological variables that are not already observable.

Regarding the avoidance of subjectivity, it is not uncommon for psychotherapists to express dissatisfaction with therapy research because of the aspiration of psychotherapy researchers to be as free of values and subjectivity as possible (e.g., Slife, Smith, & Burchfield, 2003). Indeed, many psychotherapists assert that values are an inescapable aspect of psychotherapy. Consider Burns, Goodman, and Orman (2013) in this regard:

> We suggest that psychotherapy, despite its long history to the contrary, can no longer be understood as a morally neutral or value-free practice. Many compelling arguments have been made that call psychotherapists to the recognition that psychology is implicitly and inevitably laden with moral assumptions (Dueck, 1995; Gantt & Williams, 2002; Gantt & Yanchar, 2007; Tjeltveit, 1999).
>
> (p. 2)

Or note how Harrist and Richardson (2012) make the same point by emphasizing empirical findings about the value-ladenness of psychotherapy: "numerous research studies on values and therapy over the years confirm that they are anything but value-neutral" (p. 39).

The other method features of dualism—observability and operationism—have also provoked expressions of dissatisfaction. Although these two features can be distinguished in many senses, they both depend on simplifying ecologically complex phenomena into empirical 'variables' that lead us to study only the behavioral manifestations of important phenomena of interest to psychotherapists. As Blatt, Corveleyn, and Luyten (2006) explain, for example, the "richness [of therapy] is often not reflected in empirical studies because researchers sometimes simplify concepts in an attempt to conform to more traditional methodological and theoretical points of view" (Blatt, Corveleyn, & Luyten, 2006). Or consider a similar point from Toomela (2008): "Any study of potentially causal relationships between variables can, at the best case, reveal only causal relationships between external behaviors. But not between the real objects of studies, hidden from direct observation, mental processes" (p. 260).

This situation is, in part, because "the attributes that psychometricians aspire to measure are not directly observable" (Michell, 2000, p. 648). It is also due to the translation or operationalization of the "not directly observable" into an observable operation definition (Slife, Wright, & Yanchar, 2016). As we cited Deacon (2013) earlier:

> the delivery of a fixed number of psychotherapy sessions in close adherence with a step-by-step manual, while useful in operationally defining independent variables in an RCT, bears little resemblance to routine clinical practice and is perceived by many clinicians as unduly restrictive.
>
> (p. 854)

The general upshot here regarding lawfulness and dualism is that there is an intimate connection between these method assumptions and the dissatisfaction of practicing clinicians when attempting to incorporate and apply therapy research. The lawfulness assumption seems to lead to methods and results that minimize, if not preclude, the therapeutic particular and complicated in the favor of the generalizable and simpler. The dualism assumption seems to lead to methods and results that minimize, if not preclude, the value-laden and factors, in Toomela's (2008) words, "hidden from direct observation" (p. 260) in the favor of value-free and directly observable factors.

Where to Go From Here?

There seems to be considerable evidence—with the psychotherapy literature itself as the data—that at least a portion of the dissatisfaction of therapists with therapy research is due to scientism, the exclusive focus on a particular combination of epistemological and ontological assumptions. Any combination of assumptions can become scientistic if other method assumptions are effectively excluded, either through lack of status or lack of use. However, in the case of the psychotherapy literature, a *particular* combination of empiricism and naturalism, commonly known as neopositivism, is the issue. There appears to be a disconnect between these method assumptions (and their method features) and the practice of psychotherapy that makes the findings generated through these methods difficult to apply.

This disconnect does not, of course, mean that these assumptions and their associated methods and findings are useless. Indeed, there are many therapists who would attest to their usefulness (Nelson & Steele, 2007). The issue here is the inherent limitations of these methods, like all methods, and thus the need to supplement method assumptions (and method features) for complete knowledge. Lau, Ogrodniczuk, Joyce, and Sochting (2010) describe an example of this situation. When particular therapists were faced with the problems of therapy research just outlined, they "requested more studies that used qualitative and case study methodologies, likely reflecting their desire for more 'real' research—research that gives voices to those who participate in the studies" (p. 180). Qualitative research is a good example of alternative method assumptions because much of this research, when conducted properly, originates from nonpositivist epistemologies and ontologies (Gergen, Josselson, & Freeman, 2015; Slife & Melling, 2012).

There is nothing particularly groundbreaking about the use of such 'mixed methods'. What is rarely acknowledged, however, is the extent to which each of these methods is grounded in and limited by human-made assumptions of science. Minimally, we believe, this acknowledgment would imply that these assumptions should be more explicated in research publications and considered in their evaluation. Such acknowledgment would also mean that no set of method assumptions, and thus features of methods, can claim preeminent status. RCTs, for example, are often considered the gold standard of research design (Deacon, 2013; Lilienfeld et al., 2013), yet from the perspective of a *truly* mixed set of methods, including mixed set of method assumptions, even RCTs cannot be automatically viewed as the best for any particular study or topic area without the explication of its undergirding philosophical assumptions and the justification of its methods and results.

We emphasize 'truly' in the previous sentence because mixed methods are too often thought to be merely differing method procedures (e.g., surveys vs.

interviews, number vs. words), where an actual plurality of methodologies would also imply differing method assumptions. Qualitative studies, in this sense, are too often conducted from the perspective of positivism where, for example, the researchers still insist on finding law-like and objective results. Instead, qualitative investigations should be understood to originate from, in many cases at least, radically differing assumptions, such as hermeneutics, where the assumptions of lawfulness and dualism are not presumed (Packer, 2011; Slife & Melling, 2012).

Methodological pluralism also implies an openness to other method-ologies, perhaps not yet formulated. This kind of method openness would require a reversal of the typical positivist approach to research, where the subject matter that psychologists study must be modified (operationalized) before investigation to fit the reigning method assumptions (e.g., observ-ability). A thoroughgoing methodological pluralism would first consider the nature of the phenomena to be studied and *then* choose the best method or methods for studying it (Slife & Melling, 2012; Slife & Gantt, 1999). If, for example, there are important aspects of therapy that are "not directly observable," as some therapists report (see above), then methods that do not subscribe to the epistemology of empiricism may be needed.

This pluralistic alternative to scientism may seem complicated, but it is directly analogous to a simple carpenter's toolbox. This toolbox typically has a variety of tools (or methods), because few carpenter jobs can be adequately completed with only one tool. Analogously, complete knowledge of psycho-therapy phenomena may require complementary methodologies (assumptions of methods). The advantage of carpenter tools—over the tools of a psycholog-ical researcher—is that the limits of carpenter tools are fairly easy to under-stand and then use appropriately (e.g., hammer for pounding, saw for cutting). Understanding the limits of methodological tools, however—especially if one wants to avoid scientism—requires not only the knowledge of the method assumptions that spawned them but also the possibility of viable alternatives.

Notes

1 Instead, this dissatisfaction is understood either as some failing among psychother-apists to practice in the correct 'scientific' manner (e.g., Lilienfeld, 2010; Mumma, 2014; Shean, 2013) or as some inherent problem between science and practice (e.g., Barker, Pistrang, & Elliot, 2002; Deacon, 2013; Ogrodniczuk, Piper, Joyce, Lau, & Sochting, 2010; Sobell, 2016). As we try to show, neither of these reasons is accurate because scientism itself is one root of this dissatisfaction.
2 The problem with the reification of these method features—this *process* of scientism— is that virtually everyone in the field of psychotherapy assumes that science liter-ally *is* this epistemology and metaphysic. It is as if these philosophies really aren't philosophies at all, or that these philosophies are the only choices available to any

self-respecting scientist. Qualitative research is often acknowledged, to be sure, but these methods are frequently viewed as if they originate from the same general philosophies, which itself is another sign of their reification (Slife & Gantt, 1999). Or, qualitative methods are treated as if they are merely hypothesis-generators that quantitative methods must ultimately test. In either case, the reification of method assumptions leads to the notion that qualitative methods are the poor stepchildren of therapy research, and as such not really or wholly 'scientific' (Slife & Williams, 1995; Wendt & Slife, 2007).

3 Another possible justification for scientism in the psychotherapy literature is the notion that neo-positivist method assumptions are somehow empirically supported. In other words, the success of these method features has somehow 'validated' their exclusive use. As mentioned, however, there is a "boot-strap problem" inherent in this justification (Slife & Williams, 1997), where the antiquated metaphor of straps on one's boots means that one cannot pull oneself into the air by one's own bootstraps (Slife & Williams, 1995). The meaning here is that one cannot validate or even support a method by using the method in question. It's a bit like claiming the validation of the game of Monopoly as the best of all games by only playing Monopoly. For real validation, other configurations of method features would need to be investigated, and even then the question arises as to which method features would be used for the comparison. And this boot-strap issue says nothing about the literal faith many therapy researchers have in current methods, and thus the faith they have in the philosophies that underwrite them, whether or not the method is successful.

References

American Psychological Association. (2006). Evidence-based practice in psychology. *American Psychologist, 61*(4), 271–285.

Aragona, M. (2013). Neopositivism and the DSM psychiatric classification. An epistemological history. Part 2: Historical pathways, epistemological developments and present-day needs. *History of Psychiatry, 24*(4), 415–426.

Barak, A. (1995). Empiricism, scientism, and sciolism in psychological counselling and therapy: Reaction to Martin. *Canadian Journal of Counselling, 29*(4), 308–313.

Barker, C., Pistrang, N., & Elliott, R. (2002). *Research methods in clinical psychology: An introduction for students and practitioners* (2nd ed.). West Sussex: John Wiley and Sons.

Beutler, L. E., Williams, R. E., & Wakefield, P. J. (1993). Obstacles to disseminating applied psychological science. *Applied and Preventive Psychology, 2*(2), 53–58.

Beutler, L. E., Williams, R. E., Wakefield, P. J., & Entwistle, S. R. (1995). Bridging scientist and practitioner perspectives in clinical psychology. *American Psychologist, 50*(12), 984–994.

Blatt, S. J., Corveleyn, J., & Luyten, P. (2006). Minding the gap between positivism and hermeneutics in psychoanalytic research. *Journal of the American Psychoanalytic Association, 54*(2), 571–610.

Borg, W. R., & Gall, M. D. (1989). *Educational research: An introduction* (5th ed.). New York: Longman.

Burns, J. P., Goodman, D. M., & Orman, A. J. (2013). Psychotherapy as moral encounter: A crisis of modern conscience. *Pastoral Psychology, 62*, 1–12.

Christopherson, C. (2016, November 11). Tools for progress in psychotherapy research. *Society for the Advancement of Psychotherapy.* Retrieved April 11, 2017, from http://societyforpsychotherapy.org/tools-progress-psychotherapy-research/

Clegg, J. W. (2016). Reconsidering philosophy of science pedagogy in psychology: An evaluation of methods texts. *Journal of Philosophical and Theoretical Psychology, 36*(4), 199–213.

Coaley, K. (2009). *Introduction to psychological assessment and psychometrics.* Thousand Oaks, CA: Sage.

Deacon, B. J. (2013). The biomedical model of mental disorder: A critical analysis of its validity, utility, and effects on psychotherapy research. *Clinical Psychology Review, 33*(7), 846–861.

Dueck, A. (1995). *Between Jerusalem and Athens: Ethical perspectives on culture, religion, and psychotherapy.* Grand Rapids, MI: Baker Books.

Edelson, M. (1994). Can psychotherapy research answer this psychotherapist's questions? In P. F. Talley, H. H. Strupp, & S. F. Butler (Eds.), *Psychotherapy research and practice* (pp. 60–87). New York: Basic Books.

Elliott, R., & Morrow-Bradley, C. (1994). Developing a working marriage between psychotherapists and psychotherapy researchers: Identifying shared purposes. In P. F. Talley, H. H. Strupp, & S. F. Butler (Eds.), *Psychotherapy research and practice* (pp. 124–139). New York: Basic Books.

Feyerabend, P. K. (1995). History of the philosophy of science. In T. Honderich (Ed.), *Oxford companion to philosophy* (pp. 1623–1628). New York: Oxford University Press.

Furlong, N. E., Lovelace, E. A., & Lovelace, K. L. (2000). *Research methods and statistics: An integrated approach.* New York: Harcourt College.

Gantt, E. E., & Williams, R. N. (Eds.). (2002). *Psychology for the other: Levinas, ethics, and the practice of psychology.* Pittsburgh, PA: Duquesne University Press.

Gantt, E. E., & Yanchar, S. C. (2007). Irreducible ethics: A defense of strenuousness and responsibility. *Journal of Theoretical and Philosophical Psychology, 27*(1), 35–52.

Gergen, K. J., Josselson, R., & Freeman, M. (2015). The promises of qualitative inquiry. *American Psychologist, 70*(1), 1–9.

Gyani, A., Shafran, R., Myles, P., & Rose, S. (2014). The gap between science and practice: How therapists make their clinical decisions. *Behavior Therapy, 45*(2), 199–211.

Harrist, S., & Richardson, F. C. (2012). Disguised ideologies in counseling and social justice work. *Counseling and Values, 57*(1), 38–44.

Kazdin, A. E. (2002). *Research design in clinical psychology* (4th ed.). Boston, MA: Allyn & Bacon.

Kazdin, A. E. (2007). Mediators and mechanisms of change in psychotherapy research. *Annual Review of Clinical Psychology, 3*, 1–27.

Kerlinger, F. N., & Lee, H. B. (2000). *Foundations of behavioral research.* New York: Holt, Rinehart, and Winston.

Krathwohl, D. R. (2009). *Methods of educational and social science research: The logic of methods.* Long Grove, IL: Waveland Press.

Lau, M. A., Ogrodniczuk, J., Joyce, A. S., & Sochting, I. (2010). Bridging the practitioner-scientist gap in group psychotherapy. *International Journal of Group Psychotherapy, 60*(2), 177–196.

Lilienfeld, S. O. (2010). Can psychology become a science? *Personality and Individual Differences, 49*(4), 281–288.

Lilienfeld, S. O., Ritschel, L. A., Lynn, S. J., Cautin, R. L., & Latzman, R. D. (2013). Why many clinical psychologists are resistant to evidence-based practice: Root causes and constructive remedies. *Clinical Psychology Review, 33*(7), 883–900.

Marzillier, J. (2004). The myth of evidence-based psychotherapy. *Psychologist, 17*(7), 392–395.

Michell, J. (2000). Normal science, pathological science, and psychometrics. *Theory and Psychology, 10*(5), 639–667.

Morrow-Bradley, C., & Elliott, R. (1986). Utilization of psychotherapy research by practicing psychotherapists. *American Psychologist, 41*(2), 188–197.

Mumma, G. H. (2014). Bridging the scientist–practitioner gap: Notable progress from one side. *PsycCRITIQUES, 59*(2).

Nelson, T. D., & Steele, R. G. (2007). Predictors of practitioner self-reported use of evidence-based practices: Practitioner training, clinical settings, and attitudes toward research. *Administration and Policy in Mental Health and Mental Health Services Research, 34*(4), 319–330.

Ogrodniczuk, J. S., Piper, W. E., Joyce, A. S., Lau, M. A., & Sochting, I. (2010). A survey of Canadian Group Psychotherapy Association members' perceptions of psychotherapy research. *International Journal of Group Psychotherapy, 60*(2), 159–176.

Open Science Collaboration. (2015). Estimating the reproducibility of psychological science. *Science, 349*(6251).

Packer, M. J. (2011). *The science of qualitative research.* New York: Cambridge University Press.

Privitera, G. J. (2014). *Research methods for the behavioral sciences.* Thousand Oaks, CA: Sage.

Ray, W. J. (2006). *Methods: Toward a science of behavior and experience* (8th ed.). Belmont, CA: Thompson Wadsworth.

Rieken, R., & Gelo, O. C. G. (2015). The philosophy of psychotherapy science: Mainstream and alternative views. In O. C. G. Gelo, A. Pritz, & R. Rieken (Eds.), *Psychotherapy research: Foundations, process, and outcome* (pp. 67–93). New York: Springer.

Russell, J. F. (2013). If a job is worth doing, it is worth doing twice. *Nature, 496*(7443), 7.

Schweigert, W. A. (2006). *Research methods in psychology: A handbook.* Long Grove, IL: Waveland Press.

Shean, G. D. (2013). Controversies in psychotherapy research: Epistemic differences in assumptions about human psychology. *American Journal of Psychotherapy, 67*(1), 73–87.

Slife, B. D., & Gantt, E. E. (1999). Methodological pluralism: A framework for psychotherapy research. *Journal of Clinical Psychology, 55*(12), 1453–1465.

Slife, B. D., & Melling, B. S. (2012). Method decisions: Quantitative and qualitative inquiry in the study of religious phenomena. *Pastoral Psychology, 61*(5–6), 721–734.

Slife, B. D., Reber, J. S., & Faulconer, J. E. (2012). Implicit ontological reasoning: Problems of dualism in psychological science. In R. W. Proctor & E. J. Capaldi (Eds.), *Psychology of science: Implicit and explicit reasoning* (pp. 459–478). New York: Oxford University Press.

Slife, B. D., & Slife, N. M. (2014). Empiricism. In T. Teo (Ed.), *Encyclopedia of critical psychology* (pp. 571–578). New York: Springer.

Slife, B. D., Smith, A. F., & Burchfield, C. (2003). Psychotherapists as crypto-missionaries: An exemplar on the crossroads of history, theory, and philosophy. In *About psychology: Essays at the crossroads of history, theory, and philosophy* (pp. 55–72). Albany: State University of New York Press.

Slife, B. D., & Williams, R. N. (1995). *What's behind the research? Discovering hidden assumptions in the behavioral sciences.* Thousand Oaks, CA: Sage.

Slife, B. D., & Williams, R. N. (1997). Toward a theoretical psychology: Should a subdiscipline be formally recognized? *American Psychologist, 52,* 117–129.

Slife, B. D., Wright, C. D., & Yanchar, S. C. (2016). Using operational definitions in research: A best-practices approach. *Journal of Mind and Behavior, 37*(2), 119–139.

Sobell, L. C. (2016). Bridging the gap between scientists and practitioners: The challenge before us. *Behavior Therapy, 47*(6), 906–919.

Stewart, R. E., & Chambless, D. L. (2007). Does psychotherapy research inform treatment decisions in private practice? *Journal of Clinical Psychology, 63*(3), 267–281.

Stiles, W. B. (2009). Logical operations in theory-building case studies. *Pragmatic Case Studies in Psychotherapy, 5*(3), 9–22.

Thorndike, E. L. (1940). *Human nature and social order.* New York: Palgrave Macmillan.

Tjeltveit, A. C. (1999). *Ethics and values in psychotherapy.* New York: Routledge.

Toomela, A. (2008). Variables in psychology: A critique of quantitative psychology. *Integrative Psychological and Behavioral Science, 42*(3), 245–265.

Weisz, J. R., Krumholz, L. S., Santucci, L., Thomassin, K., & Ng, M. Y. (2015). Shrinking the gap between research and practice: Tailoring and testing youth psychotherapies in clinical care contexts. *Annual Review of Clinical Psychology, 11*(1), 139–163.

Wendt, D. C., Jr., & Slife, B. D. (2007). Is evidence-based practice diverse enough? Philosophy of science considerations. *American Psychologist, 62*(6), 613–614.

7 Science and Society
Effects, Reactions, and a Call for Reformation

Jeffrey S. Reber

In February 1998, the highly respected and prestigious British medical journal the *Lancet* published a study that suggested a possible causal link between administration of the measles, mumps, and rubella (MMR) vaccine and behavioral disorders in children, with autism being the most prevalent disorder identified among the small sample used in the case series study (9 of 12 participants). Although the sample was very small, the study design lacked adequate control, and the conclusions drawn were highly speculative, the study significantly influenced the public. Rates of MMR vaccination in Britain and the United States declined as a growing number of parents became fearful about their children developing autism from the vaccine. Within a short time, several outspoken celebrities and politicians joined this growing public health scare.

Following these developments, epidemiologists began conducting and publishing studies with very large samples and more rigorous study designs that repudiated the claimed link between the MMR vaccine and autism and also pointed to a number of significant flaws in the 1998 study. Six years after the publication of the original article, 10 of its 13 authors issued a short retraction of the interpretation of the original study results. At the same time, the *Lancet* discovered that the authors failed to disclose financial interests, noting that the study's lead author, Andrew Wakefield, received funding for the research from lawyers hired by parents to conduct lawsuits against companies producing the vaccine. Finally, in 2010 the *Lancet* issued a full and complete retraction of the Wakefield, et al. article, citing a number of significant problems with the paper, including scientific misrepresentations and ethics violations. Ultimately, Britain's General Medical Council found Wakefield guilty of dishonesty and irresponsibility, and in 2011 a series of publications in the *British Medical Journal* chronicled the exposure of Wakefield et al.'s deliberate fraud for financial gain.

Despite the retraction and revelations of fraud, the administration of MMR and other vaccinations has continued to decline, incidents of measles and other preventable diseases have risen, parents' fears for their children's safety persist, and celebrity antivaccination advocacy remains (BBC, 2017; Centers for Disease Control and Prevention, 2014). Indeed, as recently as the 2016 presidential campaign, then candidate Donald Trump fanned the fires of belief about a possible link between vaccination and autism in a GOP primary debate, stating that, "Just the other day, 2 years old, 2½ years old, a child, a beautiful child went to have the vaccine, and came back, and a week later got a tremendous fever, got very, very sick, now is autistic" (Marcotte, 2015, para. 1).

Many scientists find it disconcerting that the exposure of fraud along with the self-corrective scientific measures applied to this instance of science gone wrong have not dissuaded a number of parents, celebrities, politicians, and Wakefield himself from persisting in an antivaccination campaign that has clearly been a detriment to public health. It is also troubling, as Rao and Andrade (2011) have noted, that the journal editor, peer reviewers, and readers of the journal article did not catch and correct these issues. In their words, "It is a matter of concern that the exposé was a result of journalistic investigation, rather than academic vigilance followed by the institution of corrective measures" (Rao & Andrade, 2011, para. 5). What perhaps bothers scientists most in this example and others like it is that the acceptance or rejection of the scientific claims made about these issues by various individuals and sectors within the public realm seem to have little to do with the epistemology that scientists embrace and tout as the cornerstone of their discipline: empiricism.

A Science Education Problem?

The concerns of scientists illustrated by this example may be indicative of a broader issue at play in the relationship between science and society. A recent survey conducted by the Pew Research Center and the American Association for the Advancement of Science (AAAS; 2015) found that 84% of 3,748 scientists surveyed believed that the public's knowledge of science was limited and saw this as a "major concern." It is a major concern to scientists in part because of a broadening gap between public opinion and the views of scientists. For example, while almost 90% of the scientists polled in this survey believe that genetically modified foods are safe to eat, only 37% of the 2,002 members of the public who were surveyed shared that belief. Additionally, only 50% of the public respondents agreed that "climate change is mostly due to human activity," compared to 87% of scientists. Finally, on the topic of vaccinations just discussed, 86% of scientists believe vaccinations like the MMR vaccine should be mandatory, compared to 68% of the public. It would appear that on a number of topics and issues, the American public today does not see eye to eye with scientists. And although the survey results indicate that the public's view of science generally remains "very positive" (79% of respondents), it has declined moderately in recent years.

Many scientists believe the best corrective measure to address this widening gap between public opinion and the views of scientists is an increase in science education. Indeed, 75% of the scientists surveyed by the Pew Research Center and the AAAS believe that an increase in required STEM (science, technology, engineering, and mathematics) courses in our schools would provide the best solution to the public's ignorance. But will taking more science courses resolve scientists' major concern? On the face of it, scientists' call for increased education in empirical science seems like the most reasonable solution to this problem. If the public could properly digest scientific articles and more fully understand the empirical methods used by scientists, then perhaps the public would be more likely to align its opinions with the findings of science and it would be less susceptible to misinformation.

This argument seems to make good sense. However, it is important to bear in mind that the public was not responsible for the publication of the Wakefield et al. (1998) study. Highly educated and well-trained scientists conducted the study, edited the journal *Lancet*, served as its peer reviewers, and determined whether to publish a research article or not. Moreover, as Rao and Andrade (2011) point out, it was not scientists and their corrective measures but journalists acting on behalf of the public who exposed Wakefield's financial interests and the researchers' fraudulent research. So the question remains: Is the widening gap between science and society a consequence of a public lacking in sufficient knowledge about empirical science, and will more science education create a more knowledgeable public and close the gap between public opinion and the views of scientists? This question, as scientists would likely be quick to point out, is itself an empirical question needing investigation, but to date there is no program of empirical research addressing whether more science education will narrow the gap between the views of society and those of scientists. In lieu of systematic empirical research on this question, an anecdotal illustration may provide a potentially instructive examination of this question.

An Anecdotal Illustration

In January 2017, I surveyed the 31 psychology students coming into my spring semester senior capstone course as to their science literacy. Specifically, I first provided them with the following abstract from a study that had just been published on the relationship of religious experiences to activity in areas of the brain that appear to be associated with reward (Ferguson,

Nielsen, King, Dai, & Giangrasso, 2016). I only provided the abstract because the abstract is often the only part of a published article that students have access to and/or will read (Shannon & Winterman, 2012). The abstract reads as follows:

High-level cognitive and emotional experience arises from brain activity, but the specific brain substrates for religious and spiritual euphoria remain unclear. We demonstrate using functional magnetic resonance imaging scans in 19 devout Mormons that a recognizable feeling central to their devotional practice was reproducibly associated with activation in nucleus accumbens, ventromedial prefrontal cortex, and frontal attentional regions. Nucleus accumbens activation preceded peak spiritual feelings by 1–3 s and was replicated in four separate tasks. Attentional activation in the anterior cingulate and frontal eye fields was greater in the right hemisphere. The association of abstract ideas and brain reward circuitry may interact with frontal attentional and emotive salience processing, suggesting a mechanism whereby doctrinal concepts may come to be intrinsically rewarding and motivate behavior in religious individuals.

(Ferguson, Nielsen, King, Dai, & Giangrasso, 2016, p. 1)

After reading the abstract, I asked the students to summarize in their own words the key findings of the study reported in the abstract. Eight of the students (26%) stated that they did not understand what the key findings of the study were. Seventeen (55%) attempted to summarize the key findings, but got them fundamentally wrong, as illustrated by the following response: "The key finding of the study describes how religious individuals brains may work compared to those that are not as religious" (no such comparison was described). Six of the students surveyed (19%) correctly described one or two features of the finding while incorrectly summarizing other features. One student, for example, correctly summarized the finding of an association between devotional practice and brain activity in areas of the brain associated with reward, but then mistakenly asserted that the researchers also found that religious ideas stimulated a certain moral conduct in devout people. Ultimately, none of the 31 students fully and accurately summarized the key findings of the study reported in the abstract.

Despite these difficulties in properly understanding the study findings based on their reading of the abstract and, most notably, without having read the full article, a majority of the students felt that a number of conclusions could be reasonably drawn from the study. For example, 83% of the students agreed with the conclusion that "for religious people, the same reward circuitry involved in gambling is involved in spiritual experiences."

Seventy-nine percent supported the conclusion that "it is possible for neuroscientists to study the causal mechanisms behind religious experiences by studying the brain," and 75% concluded that "fMRI [functional magnetic resonance imaging] scans can show what people are feeling." Sixty-three percent of the students agreed that "religious experience arises from brain activity," and half of the respondents supported the conclusion that this study revealed that "when a religious person says they 'feel the spirit' it is really just brain activity." When asked if they would share these conclusions with friends if a conversation on religious experience were to come up, 69% of the students indicated that they would do that—a disconcerting prospect given that none of them fully and properly understood the findings.

Finally, to assess the extent to which the students could explain several research methodology and statistical analysis concepts that would have to be understood in order to interpret the findings of this study and other psychology studies accurately, the students responded to four open-ended questions. When asked to explain the difference between random sampling and convenience sampling, only 32% of the students demonstrated a proper understanding of that difference in their responses. None of the 31 students could explain to any degree the logic of null hypothesis testing, the meaning of a reported significance test that had a p-value less than .05, or the concept of effect size and its proper interpretation when an effect size of $d = .59$ is reported.

In light of these results, it would appear, to the extent that my students represent the public, that scientists' concerns about the public's limited knowledge of science may be justified. Indeed, it might be that a large number of people in America are not capable of understanding scientific research or critically evaluating its quality. If so, then the frustration and even perturbation expressed by a number of scientists about the tendency of some sectors of the public to accept or reject the findings of science out of hand are warranted. Perhaps, then, as many scientists argue, the solution to this major concern is an increase in science education.

However, it is important to note that the 31 graduating seniors who completed this survey represent a sector of society and a proportion of college graduates that is on the high side of the science education spectrum. Indeed, 88% of these students indicated that they had taken at least seven science classes over the course of their schooling from elementary school until now, and 68% of the students responded that they had taken 10 or more science classes. Furthermore, 72% of the students had taken at least one statistics class and 60% have taken at least one research methods course. This raises the question: Is the public's limited knowledge of science a problem of too few STEM classes, as 75% of the surveyed scientists see it, or might there be other issues at play?

The Epistemology of Trust

One key issue that might be at play concerns the epistemology at the heart of the relationship between science and society, which as the historian and sociologist of science Stephen Shapin (1995) clearly states, is not empiricism:

> Most of our formal knowledge of the natural world is derived from no other source than what scientists tell us, or, more precisely, from what is told us by their apparent spokespersons: those who teach science, those who are represented as applying it in our personal domains, those who write or speak about it in the public culture. That we *have to* trust them for almost all aspects of our formal natural knowledge should also be in no doubt. For practical reasons alone we are unlikely to subject scientists' claims to effective personal skepticism. If indeed we know these things at all, we take *on faith* the principles of aerodynamics and hydrostatics, the role of DNA in heredity and development, the chemical structure of benzene. And the public 'we' includes scientists as well as the laity, for scientists are largely in the position of laypersons when it comes to the specialist knowledge of other types of scientists.
>
> (pp. 389–390)

If Shapin is correct, then the chief epistemology at play in the relationship between science and society is trust in scientists, or more precisely, trust in their witnessing. In other words, the public, which includes scientists who are not directly empirically studying the phenomenon in question, must take it on faith that the scientists engaged in the research have properly conducted their research and empirically derived (i.e., seen with their own eyes) the outcomes of the studies they conduct (Polanyi, 1958). Thus, in the case of the Wakefield et al. (1998) study, only Wakefield and his colleagues practiced empiricism. The editor, the peer reviewers, and the scientists who read about the study in the *Lancet*, as well as the public learning about the study through the media, did not have direct access to the 12 study participants and could not empirically observe their symptoms. Therefore, everyone beyond the researchers themselves, no matter how well trained in empirical science, had no choice but to act to a large degree on the epistemology of trust in Wakefield and his colleagues who alone could claim direct empirical knowledge.

This dependence on trust in scientists as witnesses is not unique to the Wakefield case. It is inevitably true of any published scientific study. Many scientists know this and have responded by trying to bring empirical observations closer to the people who review and read the studies. For example, many scientific journals now request or require that authors provide their data sets as supplementary material so editors, reviewers, and the public at large can check the data for abnormalities and run their own analyses. However, the data that study authors provide to journals will always be at least one step removed from the materials and the research participants directly observed by the researchers who conducted the study. Moreover, we now know, as some unfortunate recent examples demonstrate, that data sets can be fabricated or manipulated to appear genuinely derived from observation when they are not (Bhattacharjee, 2013). Thus, our knowledge remains necessarily, as Polanyi (1958) reminds us, very limited with regard to the actual empirical evidence:

> The amount of knowledge which we can justify from evidence directly available to us can never be large. The overwhelming proportion of our factual beliefs continue therefore to be held at second hand through trusting others, and in the great majority of cases our trust is placed in the authority of comparatively few people of widely acknowledged standing.
>
> (p. 208)

Even when data sets have been derived empirically, they are often prone to data entry errors and interpretive biases. Scientists are quick to point out that corrective empirical measures are in place to protect against such malpractices and mistakes (Kretser, Murphy, & Dwyer, 2017). For example, replication is necessary to test whether the results of any one study might be reliable and potentially valid. Unfortunately, as several recent reports indicate (e.g., Ioannidis, 2012), the corrective empirical measure of replication has not been consistently practiced, or at least it has not easily found its way to publication in the journals of several disciplines. As a result, many of the studies cited and described in the journals, textbooks, and handbooks of a discipline, including unfortunately some studies that we now know used fabricated or manipulated data, have never been tested for their replicability. Yet, textbook authors, for example, often report the findings of single studies as if they uncover general principles that strongly support theories and have meaningful practical utility.

Many of us who conduct the studies that authors cite in their textbooks know from firsthand experience that this is so. As a young doctoral student, I conducted a study in which I was the only person with direct empirical knowledge of the results because I alone ran all the research participants through the study. My faculty advisor and co-author, the journal editor and the peer reviewers who approved the publication of the study, and the textbook author who cited this study in his social psychology textbook (see Myers, 2013, p. 113) had no direct empirical knowledge of the results. Moreover, to date no published replications of the study have been conducted.

Nevertheless, the study is reported in support of the theory of confirmation bias in Myers's text without any acknowledgment of its nonreplicated status.

Recent attempts to replicate some of the better known single-study findings that have become foundational to theories in psychology and other sciences have proven unsuccessful in more than half of the cases (Open Science Collaboration, 2015), leading to a replication crisis that is particularly pronounced in psychology but afflicts medicine and the natural sciences as well (e.g., RetractionWatch, 2017). And now, given the long history of publishing these unreplicated and in some cases unreplicable study findings in handbooks and textbooks, and given the nearly universal teaching of the theories they support to multitudes of students and the public at large, it may be difficult for scientists and the authors of the original studies to acknowledge these replication issues and recalibrate their initial confidence in the findings of these unsuccessfully replicated studies. Andrew Gelman (2016), professor of statistics and political science at Columbia University, expresses his doubt about any acknowledgment and adjustment by the authors of these studies in this way: "Part of my 'pessimistic conclusions about reproducibility' come from the fact that, when problems are revealed, it's a rare researcher who will consider that their original published claim may be mistaken" (para. 7). Even if study authors did acknowledge these potential issues with their studies, would the textbooks and handbooks used to teach psychology students the theories of the discipline, which report an abundance of unreplicated study findings, undergo the requisite revisions needed to meet or at least acknowledge deficits in relation to the standard of replication?

If the Wakefield et al. (1998) exemplar provides any indication, such a broad-ranging reconsideration and revision of studies and publications of the study would appear unlikely. Indeed, even in the face of multiple replications that disproved that study's results and the finding of fraud, Wakefield, many parents, celebrities, and even high-ranking politicians continue to support the original study findings (Dodgson, 2017). Perhaps more disconcerting, Wakefield's study has been cited 308 times by scientists publishing in journals indexed by Web of Science since its retraction (RetractionWatch, 2017), which only continues to draw attention to a study that should be treated as if it was never published in the first place.

Scientists' reactions to these critical concerns and to the public's eroding agreement with and confidence in scientific claims has been mixed, but more than a few scientists have responded by reasserting the supremacy of the empirical method to other ways of knowing. For example, a 2008 *Scientific American* article, defiantly titled "Scientists Know Better Than You—Even When They're Wrong" (Minkel, 2008), pushes back strongly against any form of 'armchair science' that might be practiced by the laity and touts the epistemological power that comes with the proper application of the empirical scientific method to issues and questions. Ultimately, Minkel asserts that even when the application of the scientific method results in mistakes, empiricism will still inevitably prevail over other epistemologies in advancing knowledge. This response is understandable given the honored status many scientists give to empiricism, but it is not itself an empirical claim. It is a rhetorical claim that can only be accepted on the basis of trust. Perhaps, scientists need to consider the possibility that the public's limited knowledge is not only or even primarily an empirical matter. Perhaps there is a need, as Shapin's (1995) quote and examples like the Wakefield et al. (1998) study suggest, for an explicit critical examination of the epistemology of trust undergirding the relationship between science and society.

Lest We Forget! The Exemplar of Nazi Racial Science

The historical exemplar of Nazi racial science highlights the need for this critical examination and suggests some lessons that might be learned and usefully applied to our current circumstances. Public trust in scientists was arguably at an all-time high in the West during the first half of the 20th century (Bijker, Bal, & Hendriks, 2009). Recognizing this, the Nazis intentionally coupled their anti-Semitic ideology with the pretense of a racial science tenuously based on principles of social Darwinism in order to gain legitimacy across all sectors of society and to supplant the conventional Christian values of German culture with a science-based ethics. As Bialis (2014) describes it:

> Nazism attempted to establish a scientific ethics by means of a biopolitical radicalization of Social Darwinism. Claiming morality to be in conjunction with the laws of nature and life was to ensure its plausibility in an era that believed in scientific and technical solutions to actual or ideologically constructed social problems. The Nazi worldview was highly compatible with the intuitive worldview of many people, whom it relieved of the burden of making their own moral judgments and to whose value system it gave systematic coherence and scientific plausibility.
>
> (p. 18)

The epistemological linchpin of the Nazi's success in this endeavor was not empiricism. Then, as now, the public, including many scientists, lacked direct access to the observables of scientific studies that supposedly would have supported the principles of Nazi eugenics. The German people at the time, however, were collectively strongly authoritarian (Suedfeld & Schaller, 2002), and since science was a premier societal authority in Germany, the laity were highly likely to place their trust in science and accept claims made in its name.

As people placed their faith in Nazi scientists and the propagandists promoting their pronouncements, it became much easier to internalize the ethics of Nazi racial science and to then act on one's own initiative. There is an abundance of evidence that this internalization occurred among many people, including a sizable number of scientists and physicians living within the Reich. Physicians who volunteered to participate in the T4 euthanasia action, for example, had no need of an overseer who ordered them to sign off on the castration or killing of a physically or mentally disabled child. They acted on their own accord, believing they did so without violating their Hippocratic Oath to do no harm, because the harm they were protecting against was that which would have been done to the blood of the German people (Proctor, 1990).

Similarly, scientists within the Reich pursued research agendas that were not imposed upon them but grew out of their internalized racial ethical worldview. The Nazi psychiatrist and educational psychologist Robert Ritter and his anthropologist assistant Eva Justin, for example, sought funding from the German Association for Scientific Research to conduct studies of 'Gypsies' living in Germany to identify and rid the German population of any mixed blood that threatened the purity of the people (United States Holocaust Memorial Museum, n.d.). As a consequence of their research, Ritter and his team initiated and provided justification for the deportation and murder of thousands of Germans he and his team of social scientists designated as 'Gypsies'.

These physicians and scientists were among the most scientifically educated people in Germany at the time, yet they internalized and propagated the precepts of Nazi racial science. It seems unlikely that more classes in the empirical method of science would have deterred them from volunteering their services in the pursuit of 'racial hygiene', as many did through participation in euthanasia, castration, deportation, 'experimentation', and extermination actions taken throughout the Reich. Similarly, there is no reason to expect that increased education in STEM courses in German schools and universities would have decreased their or the public's acceptance of Nazi social Darwinism. On the contrary, it was often the most educated German citizens who led the charge of racial purification. Indeed, many of the leaders of the *Einsatzgruppen*—special military units who carried out most of the mass shootings of an estimated one million Jews just behind the front line of the army's eastern advance—were highly educated men, including one group leader who famously held two doctoral degrees (Cymet, 2010).

It is possible, as some have suggested (e.g., Adorno, Frenkel-Brunswik, Levenson, & Sanford, 1950) that the authoritarian personalities of these physicians, social scientists, and men and women of letters compromised their objectivity and their commitment to the principles of empirical epistemology, just as it compromised their ethics. However, the sociologist Zygmunt Bauman (2000) suggests there is more to the story. In his book, *Modernity and the Holocaust*, Bauman notes that "the Holocaust was not an irrational outflow of the not yet fully eradicated residues of pre-modern barbarity. It was a legitimate resident in the house of modernity; indeed one who would not be at home in any other house" (p. 17). Thus the majority of Nazis who conducted the actions of the Holocaust, he notes, did not act irrationally or in a manner that is contrary to their education in science. Instead, they applied their education to the project of social engineering in a manner consistent with other modern projects and the epistemologies supporting them. "It was the spirit of instrumental rationality, and its modern bureaucratic form of institutionalization," argues Bauman, "which made the Holocaust-style solutions not only possible, but eminently 'reasonable'—and increased the probability of their choice" (p. 18).

Thus, in some ways, Bauman suggests, the principles of modernity were not compromised by authoritarianism. On the contrary, they were actualized by Nazi scientists and physicians who voluntarily employed modernist principles and scientific methods as a reasonable justification for a program of racial hygiene that would eradicate what they saw as a major social health concern. In this sense, their increased education in modern ideals and principles, including empiricism, rationalism, science, and objectivity, did not obviate or correct for the issues at play in the public's trust of authority. On the contrary, it appears that in a number of cases it facilitated and increased the public's trust in scientists, and reinforced the confidence and trust of the scientists in themselves and each other as practitioners of an objective method that embodied modernist principles and values.

Duke philosopher Allen Buchanan (2002) drives this point home in his excellent article on social moral epistemology. He notes that the Nazis' "cooptation" of the modern institutions of science and medicine, with all the enlightened and eminently reasonable ideals they embrace, facilitated the "disabling of the virtue of sympathy among Germans," including German scientists and physicians, in large part because those institutions enjoyed a surplus of "epistemic deference" (Buchanan, 2002). Epistemic deference is, as Buchanan defines it, "the disposition to regard some other person or group of persons as especially reliable sources of truth" (p. 136). And, he states, "social institutions that recognize some persons as experts encourage this sort of deference" (p. 136). "Indeed," he concludes,

> it is difficult to imagine how the Nazis could have succeeded so well in disabling the virtues of so many people had the Nazis not been operating

in a society in which there was so much *surplus* epistemic deference to
governmental, educational, and scientific authorities.

(p. 136)

Thus it was not only the authoritarian proclivities of the German people that
contributed to a strong bond of trust in science, but also the high status of
authority granted to the institution of science and the modern ideals it represented. And as will become evident in a moment, science typically receives
an extra helping of epistemic deference beyond other societal authorities precisely because of its stance on one of those key modern ideals: objectivity.

Lessons We Can Learn

Lesson #1

Although this historical exemplar may exaggerate things to some degree
given the unique circumstances of the time, it may also be instructive. Four
particular lessons we can learn stand out. First, this illustration strongly suggests that trust in scientists is not only involved in the relationship between
science and society, but it is the primary epistemological player. As such, it
can exert a significant epistemic and ethical power upon society with, as the
historical exemplar of Nazi racial science demonstrates, consequences that
can be severe.

Lesson #2

Second, this historical exemplar also highlights an epistemological uniqueness entailed in the faith placed in scientific authority that distinguishes
science from other cultural institutions that also depend upon trust, such as
government and religion. This uniqueness is the identification of science with
objectivity and more precisely with the explicit rejection of faith in authority,
which the famous late scientist Carl Sagan (1996) describes as "one of the
great commandments of science" (p. 31). Shapin (1995) traces this identification of science with objectivity and the explicit rejection of faith in authority to the philosophies of rationalism and empiricism that undergird modern
science:

> The seventeenth-century 'moderns' enjoined those who would reform
> traditional natural knowledge and set it upon proper foundations to
> reject reliance upon authoritative ancient texts and the hearsay testi-
> mony of other people . . . The role of trust and authority was shown to
> stand against the very idea of science . . . Seventeenth-century moderns

placed the solitary knower at the center of a scientific stage where he has remained—minority academic voices notwithstanding—until the present day. From those moderns we inherit the legacy of epistemic individualism, a legacy which makes the constitutive role of trust and authority in the making of knowledge hard to see and harder still to appreciate as a virtue.

(p. 393)

Science, then, enjoys a higher degree of trustworthiness or a "surplus of epistemic deference"—to use Buchanan's (2002) terms—in comparison to other societal authorities, such as government or the church, in part because science identifies itself with the rejection of trust in authority that obviously plagues other institutions and threatens the value of their objectivity. This rejection takes place even as science implicitly depends upon that very same trust for its authoritative status in society. In the case of Nazi racial science, the identification of science with objectivity, coupled with a denial of faith in authority, allowed racial scientists to assert that it was not the dictates of Nazi ideology that required the euthanasia of disabled persons or the deportation and extermination of people with inferior or mixed blood. Such actions, Nazi scientists regularly claimed, were necessitated by the findings of the objective application of the scientific method, a method that was designed explicitly to counteract the subjective biases that adhere to epistemologies of faith and trust.

Lesson #3

This epistemological sleight of hand inevitably reinforces a form of scientism in which other ways of knowing are devalued for their lack of objectivity, while as distinguished professor of biology at the University of South Carolina, Austin Hughes (2012), describes it, "the practitioners of science" are assumed "inherently exempt, at least in the long term, from the corrupting influences that affect all other human practices and institutions" (p. 37). He judges this exemption as "at best naïve and at worst dangerous" (p. 37), and warns that

if any human institution is held to be exempt from the petty, self-serving, and corrupting motivations that plague us all, the result will almost inevitably be the creation of a priestly caste demanding adulation and required to answer to no one but itself.

(p. 37)

This creation of a "priestly caste" that enjoys a "surplus of epistemic deference" and answers only to itself clearly emerged in Nazi-controlled Europe.

Physicians like Karl Brandt, who headed the T4 euthanasia project and over-saw extermination operations at Treblinka and several other death camps, were elevated to the highest levels of government and given absolute author-ity by the Führer himself to determine the fates of hundreds of thousands of people, with complete latitude and without any fear of legal reprisal or need for ethical compunction.

The Nazis also took heavy-handed actions to denigrate alternative ways of knowing to racial science, including burning thousands of books that con-noted any disagreement with the principles of social Darwinism, eliminating exposure to or consideration of the values of alternative philosophies and worldviews from school curricula, and removing professors from their posts whose teachings were not in harmony with the principles of racial science. The Nazi agenda, represented by Hitler's deputy Rudolf Hess, who declared National Socialism as "nothing but applied biology," consistently proclaimed the supremacy of empirical science even though empiricism played virtually no epistemic role in the relationship between Nazi racial scientists and the public.

Lesson #4

Hughes (2012) pushes his critique of this path to scientism further, noting that scientists' claim to a "peculiar epistemic reliability that is lacking in other forms of inquiry" (i.e., objectivity; p. 37) may precipitate a decline in the public's capacity for skepticism and critical analysis of science. As a result, when scientists claim this "peculiar epistemic reliability," they:

> have taken the strange step of identifying that reliability with the insti-tutions and practitioners of science, rather than with any particular rational, empirical, or methodological criterion that scientists are bound (but often fail) to uphold. Thus a (largely justifiable) admiration for the work of scientists has led to a peculiar, unjustified role for scientists themselves—so that, increasingly, what is believed by scientists and the public to be 'scientific' is simply any claim that is upheld by many sci-entists, or that is based on language and ideas that sound sufficiently similar to scientific theories.
>
> (Hughes, 2012, pp. 37–38)

In the case of Nazi racial science, Hughes's (2012) concerns are on point. Nazi educators did not want a public trained in critical thinking and skeptical inquiry, so they trained students to admire and defer to scientists and they replaced standard school curricula with an explicitly anti-intellectual educa-tional agenda focused primarily on the education of character, with the most important character traits being discipline, conduct, honor, service, and devotion to the Führer. In his 1935 study of Nazi education in prewar Germany, Kandel observed:

> Formal education must accordingly be directed less to the development of the intellect and more to the strengthening of those emotions which will result in loyalty, self-sacrifice, and silent acquiescence in whatever may befall. Strength of will, joyful acceptance of responsibility, and resolution, rather than trained intellect, must be the ideals to be attained through education at all levels.
>
> (p. 158)

The result of this anti-intellectual education was not only a decreased capacity for critical analysis of scientific claims but also an increased likelihood that the claims made by racial scientists and their propagandists, whose use of language and ideas looked and sounded like science, were accepted by the German public, including other scientists, as factual. Petty and Cacioppo's (1986) Elaboration Likelihood Model demonstrates a thinking process by which an audience that cannot centrally elaborate upon and understand the claims and assertions of an argument has little choice but to rely on peripheral cues, like authoritative credentials or "language and ideas that sound sufficiently similar to scientific thinking" (Hughes, 2012, p. 38) in determining whether to accept or reject scientific claims.

Then and Now: Points of Overlap

Thankfully our circumstances today differ in many important ways from Nazi Germany, but there are some points of overlap. Most obviously, as scientists' "major concern" demonstrates and my survey of senior seminar students supports, society today is ill-equipped to understand or critically examine scientific studies. Furthermore, as the Wakefield et al. (1998) study illustrates, the public can rely on peripheral cues, like fear appeals, to accept or reject scientific claims.

We can drill down into the discipline of psychology and look for evidence of these same concerns. Specifically, by examining psychology research methods textbooks, which constitute the discipline's primary, mostly standardized resource for teaching science to psychology students, we can see how psychologists think about the relationship of science and society and how they treat the epistemology of trust in authority.

I selected two dozen of the most used research methods textbooks in psychology and reviewed them for signs of the four themes just reviewed. I found that only two textbooks examined the relationship between science and society at all, and both focused solely on the importance of critically evaluating media reports of scientific studies—neither text suggesting the value of critically examining the studies themselves nor describing in any degree how critical evaluations of media claims might be conducted. About half of the textbooks addressed trust or faith in authority as a way of knowing, but dedicated on average at most 1 page of the 500 or so total pages in each text to the topic.

Nine of the 12 texts that mention the epistemology of trust or faith in authority say nothing at all about its role in science. Instead, they treat faith in authority as a contrasting way of knowing to science, and they all criticize it and try to demonstrate its inferiority to empiricism. Two texts use the example of Galileo and the church to show how empirical science can disprove the claims of authority because it is based on objective observation rather than trust. The three texts that briefly acknowledge the role that trust in authority plays in science all promise that corrective empirical measures, like replication and peer review, protect against trust gaining a problematic foothold, after which the authors leave the matter to focus solely on empirical methods (citing unreplicated studies as they go). Cosby and Bates's (2015) research methods text demonstrates the typical treatment of authority and science, as well as the promise of objectivity and corrective empirical measures:

- "The scientific approach rejects the notion that one can accept *on faith* the statements of any authority."
- "Scientists do not accept on faith the pronouncements of anyone, regardless of that person's prestige or authority."
- "For scientists, knowledge is based primarily on observations."
- "Scientists have a 'show me, don't tell me attitude'."
- "Scientists make observations that are accurately reported to other scientists and the public. You can be sure that many other scientists will follow up on the findings by conducting research that replicates and extends these observations."
- "[Peer] review ensures that research with major flaws will not become part of the scientific literature."

(pp. 5–6)

This review of research methods textbooks is disconcerting on two fronts. First, in the case of my senior capstone students, all of the attention their research methods texts paid to teaching them the ins and outs of empirical methods seem to have had little impact on their ability to correctly interpret psychology research. Second, the epistemology of trust, which as Shapin (1995) points out is responsible for "most of our knowledge of the natural world," receives almost no attention in psychology methods texts. The attention it does receive consists primarily of denying its role in psychological science and demeaning it as a way of knowing in comparison to empiricism. A science education reformation is needed that increases the scientific literacy that scientists desire of the public, but also enables and encourages critical thinking about the role trust in science plays in the relationship between science and society.

A Call for Reformation

There are many models of reformation, but none appears to address the epistemology of trust in authority more instructively than the Protestant Reformation of the 16th century. The public at that time had no direct access to the origins of papal edicts and the pronouncements of priests. They depended almost entirely upon religious authorities for their understanding of scripture and their path to salvation. Reformers like Martin Luther could see the limitations of this epistemology and the corrupting implications that could and did sometimes ensue from it. Part of Luther's response to these issues was to make the Bible directly accessible to as many people as possible so they could see and know the Good Word for themselves and no longer rely on the claims of others, even well-intended and credible others.

However, the translation of the Bible into German was not Luther's first or most impactful act of reformation. His first and most influential act was an act of critical thinking, expressed through the publication of his "95 Theses," which he wrote as an invitation to church leaders to a debate concerning a list of questions and propositions about church authority and the people. Importantly, Luther's tone in this document was invitational and not accusatory, but his questions were provocative. History shows that the response from church leaders was not positive, but within 2 months, Luther's friends translated his "95 Theses" from Latin into German and then printed and distributed them to the public. Within just 8 weeks, the theses had spread throughout Europe. Based on the significant impact of the theses on the public, Luther continued the practice of printing and distributing his critical thinking on these matters, ultimately publishing more works than the next 17 most prolific reformers combined.

Luther's two reformation actions suggest a model for a scientific education reformation. First, just as Luther made the Bible more accessible to common people by translating it into the language of their understanding, scientists can make their study findings more directly accessible to the public. Scientists could do at least two things to improve this accessibility. They can replace complicated technical jargon and exotic statistical analyses with clear language and straightforward descriptions of data that make it possible for readers to process study findings centrally, rather than having to rely on peripheral cues. Additionally, they can clearly distinguish reports of their empirical observations from statements of personal belief, the consensus of scientists, and other nonempirical claims. This is important because readers, especially those who cannot centrally process the report, may take scientists' assertions and claims as empirical findings simply because they appear in a scientific paper, as was the case for a number of people, including some scientists, who read Wakefield's unjustified assertion of a causal link between the MMR vaccine and autism. If we revisit the abstract that my senior capstone students struggled to understand, we can see that both of these issues just described are prevalent and unaccounted for. In Figure 7.1, I have highlighted a few of the more obvious examples of these concerns.

A second science education reformation action that follows Luther's model would be to actively and regularly publish critical analyses of science and the epistemology of trust undergirding its relationship with society. This would be particularly important in disciplines that downplay or even deny the role of trust in scientific authority in the science of the discipline, as was the case in many of the psychology research methods textbooks I reviewed. In many scientific disciplines, including my discipline of psychology, theoretical and critical scientists are already leading the way in this critical thinking endeavor. However, their good work does not always enjoy widespread exposure within their discipline, which can limit its influence on the scientific authorities within that field.

There are two lessons from Luther's reformation that might improve the exposure and impact of these critical thinking efforts. First, like Luther,

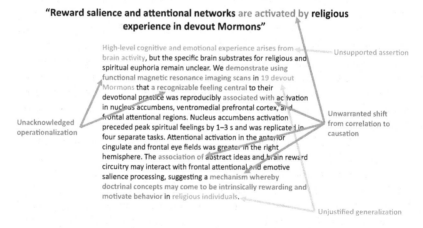

Figure 7.1 Examples of Unacknowledged Bias in Abstract From Ferguson et al. (2016)

we can write our '95 theses' in a manner that is not accusatory but rather humbly invites our peers to dialog. Authorities of any kind can be defensive and resistant to criticism, and with articles titled "Scientists Know Better Than You Do—Even When They're Wrong" (Minkel, 2008) out there, it is likely that this might be the case with some of the scientific authorities in our disciplines. Indeed, if the church authorities of Luther's time bear any resemblance to the scientific authorities in a given discipline, then it is quite possible that those authorities will disregard an invitation to critical dialog, even if it is humbly extended, and the critical analyses will be rejected or relegated to specialized journals with low readership.

However, Luther's example also shows that even if that were to occur, this invitational, humble style of critique can make great headway and establish a meaningful resonance with another important audience: the public. Just as Luther's friends saw the potential value of his humbly offered theses for the public sphere, so too can the authors of critical analyses humbly invite the public into dialog by offering their publications to the laity. If theoretical and critical scientists engage the public in dialog with them and the public learns to think more critically about science and any potential surplus of epistemic deference it enjoys, then the public can more effectively identify any tendencies toward scientism that might be present in its relationship with science. A society informed in this way can then better engage scientists in critical dialog that can promote a science education reformation that addresses all the relevant epistemologies.

Second, if this dialog with the public is going to succeed, then critical and theoretical scientists must take care to translate their critical evaluations of scientific authority into a language that the public can understand, just as Luther's friends translated his Latin version of the theses into the language spoken by the common people. Once translated into an accessible language, theoretical and critical scientists can then publish their work broadly across all strata of society. Three obvious publication outlets immediately come to mind. Most obviously, in addition to the bread and butter of traditional journal articles, theoretical and critical scientists can publish books, handbooks, and even perhaps picture and storybooks as companion volumes to traditional science education texts to teach the public to think critically about both empiricism and trust in scientific authority early and often in their education.

Another outlet, reminiscent of the newly developed technology of the printing press that Luther used in his time to reach a wider audience more quickly, is the internet. Theoretical and critical scientists can take advantage of this still recent invention and the many social and educational media capabilities it provides to spread critical thinking about science and its relationship with society broadly and rapidly. Finally, the students critical and theoretical scientists teach can carry the critical thinking skills they learn in their classes into their various circles of influence. Imagine, for example, a former student of a critical scientist who becomes a theoretically informed 4th grade teacher. Perhaps, when introducing the scientific method to her students for the first time in their lives, she also helps them begin to think critically at an age appropriate level about the ways of knowing entailed in science, including trust in scientists as authorities. Maybe, she even does that with the help of a text written for elementary students by her professor or another theoretical and critical scientist. The public outlets and possibilities for dialog are myriad, but suffice it to say for now that critical and theoretical experts in all scientific disciplines are well positioned to follow Luther's reformation model and take the lead in initiating a much-needed scientific education reformation.

Conclusion

Why do this? Why put effort into a reformation that will be challenging and may not succeed? Consider once again the model of Luther's reformation, and also another Martin Luther who initiated a reformation addressing governmental authority in relation to race and poverty in America half a millennium later. Both of these Martin Luthers endeavored to liberate the laity from ignorance and oppression by laying bare key ethical issues at play in the relationship between society and institutions of authority. They applied their own critical thinking to these issues, and they taught others how to think critically about the morality of this relationship as well. This education of the public was of critical importance to Martin Luther King Jr. (1947), who wrote that "the function of education is to teach one to think intensively and to think critically" (para. 3).

Our circumstances today are certainly not as severe as they were at the time of either of these two reformations, and I have no intention of drawing direct comparisons between the societal authorities of those times and the institution of science today. Nonetheless, one cannot help but think about the relationship between science and society as one that is inherently ethical. And, it is in the ethics-based spirit of both Luthers' reformation efforts that I believe scientists share an obligation to enable a more educated public that can examine scientific studies and reports centrally, and thereby help the public think critically and act rightly in relation to scientific authority.

References

Adorno, T. W., Frenkel-Brunswik, E., Levinson, D. J., & Sanford, R. N. (1950). *The authoritarian personality*. New York: W. W. Norton.
Bauman, Z. (2000). *Modernity and the Holocaust*. Ithaca, NY: Cornell University Press.

BBC. (2017, March). Measles outbreak across Europe. *BBC News: Health*. Retrieved September 21, 2017, from www.bbc.com/news/health-39419976

Bhattacharjee, Y. (2013). The psychology of lying: Diederik Stapel's audacious academic fraud. *New York Times*. Retrieved March 10, 2017, from www.nytimes. com/2013/04/28/magazine/diederik-stapels-audacious-academic-fraud.html

Bialis, W. (2014). Nazi ethics and morality: Ideas, problems and unanswered questions. In W. Bialis & L. Fritze (Eds.), *Nazi ideology and ethics* (pp. 15–56). Cambridge: Cambridge University Press.

Bijker, W. E., Bal, R., & Hendriks, R. (2009). *The paradox of scientific authority: The role of scientific advice in democracies*. Cambridge, MA: MIT Press.

Buchanan, A. (2002). Social moral epistemology. *Social Philosophy and Policy, 19*, 126–152.

Centers for Disease Control and Prevention. (2014, May). Measles cases in the United States reach 20-year high. *CDC Newsroom*. Retrieved September 21, 2017, from www.cdc.gov/media/releases/2014/p0529-measles.html

Cosby, P. C., & Bates, S. C. (2015). *Methods in behavioral research* (12th ed.). New York: McGraw-Hill.

Cymet, D. (2010). *The Holocaust, the Third Reich, and the Catholic church*. New York: Lexington Books.

Dodgson, L. (2017). Trump has suggested vaccines cause autism—an idea that couldn't be more wrong. *Business Insider*. Retrieved September 21, 2017, from www.businessinsider.com/trump-vaccines-autism-wrong-2017-1

Ferguson, M. A., Nielsen, J. A., King, J. B., Dai, L., Giangrasso, D. M., Holma, R., . . . Anderson, J. S. (2016). Reward, salience, and attentional networks are activated by religious experience in devout Mormons. *Social Neuroscience, 13*(1), 104–116.

Gelman, A. (2016). Replication crisis crisis: Why I continue in my "pessimistic conclusions about reproducibility." *Statistical Modeling, Causal Inference, and Social Science*. Retrieved September 21, 2017, from http://andrewgelman. com/2016/03/05/29195/

Hughes, A. L. (2012). The folly of scientism. *New Atlantis: A Journal of Technology & Society*, 32–50.

Ioannidis, J.P.A. (2012). Why science is not necessarily self-correcting. *Perspectives on Psychological Science, 7*, 645–654.

Kandel, I. L. (1935). Education in Nazi Germany. *Annals of the American Academy of Political and Social Science, 182*, 153–163.

King, M. L., Jr. (1947). The purpose of education. *Maroon Tiger*. Retrieved September 21, 2017, from www.drmartinlutherkingjr.com/thepurposeofeducation.htm

Kretser, A., Murphy, D., & Dwyer, J. (2017). Scientific integrity resource guide: Efforts by federal agencies, foundations, nonprofit organizations, professional societies, and academia in the United States. *Critical Reviews in Food Science and Nutrition, 57*(1), 163–180.

Marcotte, A. (2015, September). Donald Trump uses GOP debate to push anti-vaccination myths. *Slate.com*. Retrieved March 10, 2017, from www.slate.com/ blogs/xx_factor/2015/09/16/donald_trump_suggested_vaccines_cause_autism_ during_the_cnn_gop_debate_he.html

Minkel, J. R. (2008). *Scientists know better than you—even when they're wrong: Why fallible expertise trumps armchair science—a Q&A with sociologist of science Harry Collins*. Retrieved September 30, 2017, from www.scientificamerican.com/article/scientists-know-better-than-you/

Myers, D. G. (2013). *Social Psychology* (11th ed.). New York, NY: McGraw-Hill.

Open Science Collaboration. (2015). Estimating the reproducibility of psychological science. *Science, 349.*

Petty, R. E., & Cacioppo, J. T. (1986). The elaboration likelihood model of persuasion. *Communication and Persuasion*, 1–24.

Pew Research Center. (2015). *Public and scientists' views on science and society.* Retrieved October 1, 2017, from www.pewinternet.org/files/2015/01/PI_Science andSociety_Report_012915.pdf

Polanyi, M. (1958). *Personal knowledge: Towards a post-critical philosophy*. Chicago, IL: University of Chicago Press.

Proctor, R. (1990). *Racial hygiene: Medicine under the Nazis*. Cambridge, MA: Harvard University Press.

Rao, R.S.S., & Andrade, C. (2011). The MMR vaccine and autism: Sensation, refutation, retraction, and fraud. *Indian Journal of Psychiatry, 53*, 95–96.

Retraction Watch. (2017). *The 2017 Retraction Watch Year in Review*. Retrieved January 15, 2018, from https://retractionwatch.com/2017/12/29/2017-retraction-watch-year-review-hint-database-nearly-done/

Sagan, C. (1996). *The demon-haunted world: Science as a candle in the dark*. New York: Ballantine Books.

Shannon, S., & Winterman, B. (2012). Student comprehension of primary literature is aided by companion assignments emphasizing pattern recognition and information literacy. *Issues in Science and Technology Librarianship, 68*(4). Retrieved October 1, 2017, from www.istl.org/12-winter/refereed3.html

Shapin, S. (1995). Trust, honesty, and the authority of science. In R. Bulger, E. Meyer Bobby, & H. Fineberg (Eds.), *Society's choices: Social and ethical decision making in biomedicine* (pp. 388–408). Washington, DC: National Academy Press.

Suedfeld, P., & Schaller, M. (2002). Authoritarianism and the Holocaust: Some cognitive and affective implications. In L. Newman & R. Erber (Eds.), *Understanding genocide: The social psychology of the Holocaust* (pp. 68–90). Oxford: Oxford University Press.

United States Holocaust Memorial Museum. (n.d.). *Dr. Robert Ritter: Racial science and "Gypsies."* Retrieved March 1, 2017, from www.ushmm.org/learn/students/learning-materials-and-resources/sinti-and-roma-victims-of-the-nazi-era/dr.-robert-ritter-racial-science-and-gypsies

Wakefield, A. J., Murch, S. H., Anthony, A., Linnell, J., Casson, D. M., & Malik, M. (1998). Ileal-lymphoid-nodular hyperplasia, non-specific colitis, and pervasive developmental disorder in children (Retracted). *Lancet, 351*, 637–641.

8 Beyond Scientism

Reaches in Psychology Toward a Science of Consciousness

Frederick J. Wertz

Nothing has been more important to the definition and identity of psychology than its being a science. What a momentous error it would be if psychologists were mistaken about the nature and requirements of science! The chapters in this volume demonstrate precisely such a long-standing, pervasive error. Ironically, in its effort to be scientific, psychology has 'lost its phenomena' and, due to its inadequate conception of science, has become pseudoscientific. The error is that psychology has assumed a dogmatic and problematic ideology called 'scientism'. The distinction between scientism and genuine science is crucial. Documented in this volume are some of the complex, multifaceted, and historically intransigent ways in which psychology has employed conceptions of science without critical analysis of their assumptions and ramifications. By offering an understanding of various forms of scientism and an analysis of how they obfuscate and vitiate the possibility of genuine psychology, this volume provides the tools to identify and overcome prevailing restrictions and pretensions in order to make psychology a more authentic scientific discipline.

Daniel N. Robinson clearly articulated the fundamental issue: Psychology must not mistake or lose sight of the reality of its subject matter, mental life. Whereas an exclusive focus on and reduction to physical reality has produced great success in the natural sciences, this practice turns away from and is tantamount to the very loss of mental life as such. Methods that have been useful and knowledge that has been valid in the natural sciences may appear to be scientific in themselves, due to their familiar meaning of being 'scientific', but they miss the mark in psychology. Whether seeking knowledge about Mary's perception of the blue sky or about the creative processes and products of artists and engineers, psychology can achieve scientific status only by offering knowledge of mental life as such, not knowledge of contextless stimuli or neurophysiological processes and events, even given its legitimacy in physics and biology. Robinson's analysis of the Mary problem demonstrates how the physical reductionism characteristic of scientism excludes the very subject matter of psychology, even the most elemental realities of psychophysics: color, sound, and pain.

Richard N. Williams showed that if psychologists assume, with Hempel, that all science offers general laws of antecedent conditions and consists of testing hypothetico-deductive explanatory models, psychology runs the risk of bypassing and remaining ignorant of what it is attempting to explain. Probabilistic analyses supporting causal inferences and their mathematically formulated laws cannot offer knowledge of social life, which inextricably involves meaning. Mental life is an irreducible reality that requires description and understanding as the foundation of its science, which requires natural language. All explanations refer back to what is being explained and require placing that 'what' at the center of science, so that it can be rigorously known in its own right. Science conceived as knowledge of explanatory causal laws excludes knowledge of its 'what' and therefore lacks a foundation.

James T. Lamiell demonstrated the importance of conceptual critique and analysis in psychology. He contrasted Wundt's engagement with philosophy and his grasp of central conceptual issues that require diverse research methods with psychology's attention to the purely technical aspects of method. Ironically, the statistical analyses of aggregate data in personality research yields knowledge that is uninterpretable at the level of individual persons. The results of correlational analysis do not offer one iota of knowledge of even one participant in the research, let alone persons in the population beyond the study. Lamiell credibly asserts that statisticism—using statistics as the means of knowing lawfulness—is the single most widespread form of scientism in psychology.

Lisa M. Osbeck informed us that scientism stems from inadequate conceptions of science that unnecessarily restrict scientific rationality. Her analysis of 'intuition' in science explodes stereotypes and received knowledge of science. Just as the previous chapters found edification in Aristotle, Hayek, and Wundt and Stern, Osbeck employed a far-reaching history of ideas to broaden our understanding of rational intuition. Osbeck's placement of the acting person, including emotion and values, at the center of all scientific practice undercuts the distinction of human and natural sciences as well as quantitative and qualitative reasoning. Rational intuition, employed as genuine scientific activity in its various forms, apprehends the world of objects, various kinds of phenomena (mental and physical), general laws, relational structures, conditions of possibility, and the utterly individual. Osbeck thereby provides us with a blueprint for universal scientific rationality that is capable of providing knowledge not merely of the physical world but of subjectivity, which she reveals to lie at the center of scientific practice itself.

Edwin E. Gantt raised questions about the limited place of science in human affairs, as well as unnecessary restrictions on science in psychology.

The face of scientism revealed here is its presumed superiority, indeed its arrogant claim to be the preeminent access to reality, with all other means being riddled with illusions and falsehood. It is not uncommon for psychologists to view science as superior to all other forms of knowledge (e.g., philosophy, literature, religion, fine arts), professional expertise (e.g., of physicians, lawyers, psychologists), and personal experience, a belief that ironically does not avail itself to scientific test and that reveals scientism as a dogmatic ideology taken purely on faith, indeed the very antithesis of genuine science. Moreover, evolutionary psychology provides an example of multidimensional scientism, threatening to take over all subject matters and approaches to psychology. In principle dismissing meaning, value, purpose, and the entire realm of the mental, evolutionary psychology demands a restriction of science to causal explanatory laws, physicalistic reductionism, and quantitative analytic methods.

Brent D. Slife and his colleagues Eric A. Ghelfi and Sheilagh T. Fox carefully traced the perennial gap between science and clinical practice to uncritically assumed restrictions of scientism in psychology. Clinical science researchers and the powerful National Institute of Mental Health (NIMH) assume that the randomized controlled trial (RCT), as used in medicine, is the gold standard research design for empirically investigating the value and worth of psychotherapies. Further, they traced out the significant backlash and opposition to this way of legitimating "empirically supported treatments" to the problems of scientism, which marginalizes the importance of clinical experience, professional expertise, the interpersonal therapeutic alliance, and the individuality of patients in clinical practice. Slife et al. argued that the restrictions of scientism preclude a resolution of this debate because any constructive alternative that integrates science and practice requires a science capable of fidelity to the psychological and social phenomena of therapy. Methodological pluralism in science, including qualitative research of therapy, is offered as a constructive scientific alternative to scientistic restrictions on research methods.

Jeffrey S. Reber called attention to the gap between science and public opinion, a gap scientists attempt to close by greater focus on empirical research in education. Reber cast doubt on this as a viable solution by pointing out the deficient scientific literacy on the part of even students with substantial science education. He pointed out that despite lacking literacy, the public nonetheless trusts science, thereby ironically embodying the very faith in authority that science opposes. Reber provided dramatic evidence of the untrustworthiness of science in his examination of Nazi research, which assumed the principles of scientism without ethical constraint. When science in principle excludes the veridicality of ethical criticism from outside itself—human wisdom and philosophical reasoning—it risks harming the world, as history shows us. Scientists are human and vulnerable to social influences as well as prejudices, and a scientific establishment unaccountable to other ways of knowing, including reflection on morality and social responsibility, can be dangerous. The antidote, for Reber, is a reformation in education that features a critical understanding of science, including the unnecessary limits of scientism and nonscientific study of ethics, ontology, and epistemology.

In drawing together the insights of these various authors, the following basic points may be concluded:

1. Scientism excludes the proper subject matter of psychology—mental life—from the potential reach and scope of science.
2. Saving the phenomena of psychology requires a critical analysis and elimination of scientism and an insistence on the irreducible reality of mental life.
3. Genuine psychological science requires multiple research methods, including qualitative methods capable of all types of intuition rigorously employed in understanding and reflecting on the lives of individual persons.
4. The move beyond scientism yields knowledge of science itself as a personal project, including teleology, meaning, emotions, values, and communal practices.
5. Science can have a virtually unlimited and universal reach with proper ontological and epistemological grounding, but these require critical philosophical reflection that lies beyond the field of psychology, a situation demanding a recognition of its own limits, the basis of historical abuses of privilege, and inadequacy in the face of the intrinsic mystery of reality.
6. Even at its most authentic, science requires humility, egalitarian openness, and accountability rather than assumed superiority in relation to humanities, the arts, professional expertise, and personal experience.

As several of the authors in this volume acknowledge, the critique of scientism has been articulated with erudition and sophistication consistently for well over 100 years—virtually as long as psychology has attempted to function as a discipline independent of philosophy. Indeed the very founders of European and American psychology, Wundt and James, understood and insisted on a specific multimethod approach that would save the phenomena of mental life while maintaining a lively connection with philosophy and other disciplines. Brentano (1973) and Dilthey (1977) gave voice to these issues in the 19th century, and there have been continuing criticisms and calls for a genuine psychology that includes experience and maintains a vital link to philosophy in every decade since its founding, as Giorgi (1970) has shown. What can we now do to resolve this perennial problem? Is the situation so bleak that more than 100 years of clarity will continue to be ignored?

The aim of this volume is to liberate science from scientism. This aim, not to undermine but to purify and extend science in the service of science as science, is both negative and positive. This is an effort to remove from science its inappropriate metaphysical commitments, its restrictive methodological orthodoxy, and its unjustified hubris. As we have seen, removing ideological dogmatism is the most crucial for psychology of all scientific disciplines, because psychology is rendered impossible both in principle and in practice to the extent that it is infused with the metaphysics of materialism and the epistemology of hypothetico-deductive model testing. Inasmuch as psychology is a positive science focused on a particular region of existence, it is rightfully to be differentiated from philosophy and metaphysics as well as from physical science. Philosophy is a task for philosophers, who are trained in matters of ontology and epistemology. Physicists, chemists, and biologists are the experts in knowing the material world. Science has but one aim and obligation: to achieve knowledge that is faithful to its subject matter. The achievement of this aim, however, requires conceptual and methodological creativity and expansiveness unrestricted by prejudice and preconceptions. The rejection of scientism can free psychology to develop as a genuine science of mental life, rather than being confined to mimicry of physical science, which can only amount to psychology being a pseudoscience of mental life.

In order to become a genuine science, psychology also requires the removal of the methodological orthodoxy that privileges methods that aim at explanation by causal laws, for psychology requires, first and foremost, methods capable of offering knowledge of what mental life is, in all its various kinds. The methods required for this task, in contrast to those that test hypotheses derived from explanatory models by measurement and quantitative analysis, are *qualitative*, focused on the 'what' of mental phenomena. Quantitative psychology needs knowledge of what is being measured and of the meanings of differences in analytic results. With this we have already begun to explicate the positive gain for psychology and for science of the removal of scientism from science: A genuine psychology gains methods that allow the proper conceptualization followed by extensive, valid knowledge of its unique subject matter. Psychology free of scientism becomes objective in the most important sense, that is, capable of achieving knowledge of its proper object, the irreducible reality of mental life. In this way, the purging of scientism from science clears the way for science to be more universal by extending its reach beyond physical nature to other regions of existence, in particular to the individual person including consciousness as such.

The liberation of science from scientism also enables us to understand science more adequately—that is, as a human project infused with the subjectivity of the scientist, including basic processes of perceiving the world, adopting particular vocational attitudes, handling instruments, identifying phenomena and research problems, reasoning qualitatively and quantitatively, communicating with ordinary and mathematical languages, and participating in the community of scientists. A genuine psychology becomes capable of offering objective knowledge of the undeniably personal nature science (Osbeck, Nersessian, Malone, & Newstetter, 2011). Beyond this gain for psychology, which is also a gain for science, the liberation of science from scientism opens the way for other scientific disciplines to shed light on science, for instance by means of the philosophy of science, the sociology of science, the history of science, and the politics of science, which bring into view both the transcendental (in the case of philosophy) and human (in the case of the social sciences) aspects of science in order to provide a more adequate and objective account not only of natural science but of the entire family of sciences themselves. With their distinctive methods, sciences are capable of studying each other, yielding not only the philosophy of metaphysics and ethics and the chemistry of the brain but also a history of biology, a sociology of philosophy, a political science of psychology, and so on. Freed from scientism, the sciences become differentiated according to the essential demands of their objects, their subject matter, without reducing one subject matter to another and each offering its own unrestricted and original contributions.

The differentiation and extension of the sciences afforded by their freedom from scientism by no means implies their incommensurability. On the contrary, distinct sciences pursuing the unique demands of their own subject matters is the precondition for genuine interdisciplinarity. In the case of psychology, for instance, rather than being swallowed up by evolutionary biology or by neuroscience—as scientism currently threatens—psychologists would be able to collaborate with evolutionary biologists and neuroscientists by offering clearer knowledge of psychological processes that may be related to evolution and the brain as known by biologists. Sound disciplines without boundary violations are a prerequisite for interdisciplinary collaboration through team science.

Liberating science from scientism, in part thanks to the broad and variegated scientific knowledge thereby generated and the enhanced understanding of science itself, teaches us that there is more to life than science. Everyday human experience and nonscientific disciplines in the humanities and fine arts have value in their own right and offer knowledge that cannot properly be subordinated to science but rather stands alongside science, in the fullness of life, with their own importance and dignity. They offer an invaluable perspective on science. Moreover, science itself is based on prescientific experience and, indeed, presupposes it. The understanding of science in the context of existence in its fullness, as one kind of human activity, bestows on science a healthy humility and places it in a position to both teach and learn from nonscientific regions of everyday life, such as religions, the humanities, and the arts, with which science has more in common, and a potentially more fruitful interchange, than follows from the presumptuous imperialistic dogma of scientism.[1] The best science respectfully assumes accountability to the whole of variegated humanity.

The liberation of psychology from scientism by no means imposes a new agenda on psychology. Rather, the discipline of psychology in its struggle for scientific authenticity has already been enacting this liberation throughout its historical trajectory, with positive gain, although the theoretical and methodological advances afforded have not necessarily been understood as overcoming scientism. These advances have been accomplished by using the very practices of rational intuition, so necessary for all sciences, that were articulated by Osbeck in this volume (see also Osbeck & Held, 2014). On a relatively large and self-conscious scale, such movements include phenomenological psychology (Wertz, 2006), which has been developing as an antidote to naturalism since the early 20th century, and humanistic psychology (Wertz, 1998), which emerged in mid-century as a critique of dehumanization and a restoration of the person in psychology and continues to flourish today. Such gains are also abundantly available within psychoanalysis, learning theory, cognitive psychology, experimental psychology, biological psychology, and psychological research methodology.

Psychoanalysis began with Freud's advance in psychopathology beyond the physicalistic reduction by neurology with his discovery of the psychogenesis of the mental disorders of his time, whose properly psychological study led Freud to the phenomenon of meaning as evident in personal history and culture (Wertz & Olbert, 2016). Drawing on his background as a physical scientist, natural science theorizing was always a part of Freud's work, most explicitly in his 1895 unfinished and unpublished "Project for a Scientific Psychology," a project with a naturalistic conception of that bears no resemblance to any of Freud's further contributions of the next 40 years (Freud, 1977). On the contrary, all Freud's observations, analyses, and generation of new knowledge were genuinely psychological. Psychoanalysts have accomplished and recognized a consistent movement from physicalistic and biologistic theoretical constructs (e.g., energy, instinct, homeostatic reduction) to theory featuring distinctively personal concepts (meaning, intention, purpose, and object relations) within Freud's work and consistently in virtually every advance during the 20th century (Guntrip, 1971). Contemporary psychoanalysis emphasizes relationality (Mitchell & Aron, 1999) and intersubjectivity, explicitly utilizing phenomenological philosophy (Atwood & Stolorow, 1984).

Learning theory began from a perspective of extreme scientism in its postulation of causal stimulus-response laws of classical conditioning, as a universal explanatory model of all psychological phenomena (Watson, 1925).
Skinner's advance in operant conditioning moved away from Watson's
physicalism by viewing the organism as the initiator of behavior and the
environment not as stimuli but in its functional relations with the behavior,
such that persons are cultural beings who shape the world as they are shaped
by it (Skinner, 1971).[2] Based partly on Rotter's introduction of subjective
expectancy into learning (1954), Bandura (1977) theorized learning as a
social, cognitive, and agentic process of reciprocal determinism. In learning
theory, we see a movement from causal explanation with physical reductionism to the conceptualization of mental life as distinctly human, social, and
agentic.

Cognitive psychology, having reintroduced mental life in psychology
after it had long been banished by behaviorism, and neuroscience, as it rises
to ever-greater prominence among the sciences, has recently been opening
generative dialogues with phenomenological philosophers by developing
forward-moving theories of embodied, embedded, enactive, and extended
cognition (Baerveldt & Verheggen, 1999; Hall & Nemirovsky, 2012;
McGann, De Jaegher & Di Paolo, 2013).[3]

Research methodology is the stronghold of scientism in psychology.
Even in this area, there have been continuous advances involving qualitative methods that neither test hypothetical explanations nor establish causal
laws. Although recognized only recently, the creative utilization of qualitative methods in psychology has been responsible for generating original
knowledge in virtually all fields ranging from psychopathology to developmental, motivational, personality, social, and cognitive psychology (Wertz,
2014). The first formal qualitative method was developed by the psychome-
trician John Flanagan (1954), who later became president of the American
Psychological Association's (APA) Division of Evaluation, Measurement,
and Statistics, and whose qualitative Critical Incident Technique (drawing
on professional psychologists' experiences) has been used as the basis of
the APA's first and subsequent ethics codes. The research by Piaget and
Kohlberg in developmental psychology and Nobel Prize winners Simon
and Kahneman exemplify the significance of utilizing qualitative methods
in psychology (Wertz, 2014). More systemically, beginning in the 1980s
the almost exclusive formal emphasis on measurement and statistical analyses in psychology has given way to the very methodological pluralism that
Slife et al. call for (see also Wertz, 2011). This development is reflected in
the inclusion of the Society for Qualitative Inquiry in Psychology in APA
Division 5, which changed its name from "Evaluation, Measurement, and

Statistics" to "Quantitative and Qualitative Methods in Psychology" (Freeman & Wertz, 2012).[4]

Given the pervasiveness of scientism in psychology, it could well be argued that genuine progress in psychology throughout its history has consistently involved the liberation of psychological science from scientism. However, can we count on psychology to continue to liberate itself from scientism? Reber rightly points out that the orthodoxy of scientism is and remains firmly entrenched in our research methods education. Although many textbooks and courses on qualitative methods, including lively attention to philosophy, are becoming more common, much of the research methods curriculum remains steeped in scientism, and dogmatic coverage of research methods is perhaps even more extreme in introductory textbooks in psychology. One popular introductory text that was recently adopted for all courses in my department is *Psychology: From Inquiry to Understanding* by Lilienfeld, Lynn, and Namy (2018). Not only is coverage of the qualitative revolution absent in this textbook, but qualitative research, usually in the form of case studies, is relegated to the bottom of the methodological hierarchy, considered to be little better than anecdotes. Moreover, the only use of case studies is in generating hypotheses that, in order to gain scientific status, need to be converted into causal explanations yielding hypotheses tested by the very quantitative, aggregate analyses that Lamiell shows miss the individual person, the subject matter of psychology. Throughout this text, and indeed in every chapter, the true (randomized, controlled) experiment is lauded as the gold standard, indeed the only method capable of supporting a causal inference, and causal explanation is considered synonymous with scientific knowledge. Arguments waged for more than 150 years, underlined by Allport (1942) and regularly reiterated by qualitative methodologists, that causal explanation is inappropriate in psychology are not considered, and therefore qualitative research methods are considered valuable only as a preliminary stage of scientific investigation that must always be surpassed by experimental validation of causal inferences. New work that accepts hypothesis testing quantitative research and integrating it with qualitative methods (Creswell, Klassen, Piano Clark, and Clegg Smith, 2011) is not mentioned in this text, let alone considered a fruitful integration of methods with future promise.

What about the other mainstay of scientism: physicalistic reductionism? Where does the Lilienfeld et al. (2018) text stand on that? This textbook includes and reflects many studies of genuine psychological processes that are not in any way reduced to neurology, demonstrating that there is much uniquely psychological research developing in our field. Many of the advances toward genuine psychology noted earlier are reflected in this text. Stress, along with many phenomena, is considered "a subjective experience"

(p. 456). Relational processes such as when a person "tends and befriends" threatening situations (p. 459) are commonly reported. Voluminous research is reported on the value of strong interpersonal relationships (p. 461), agentic control of one's environment (pp. 461–463), commitment to life and work (p. 464), flexible ways of coping (p. 465), and even spirituality (p. 465)— all properly psychological. However, expansive coverage of neuroscience is prominently featured in every chapter and is considered identical with psychology. In fact, the authors consistently assume throughout the text that mental life and the brain are identical, revealing the assumption that warrants the equation of neuroscience and psychology and the lack of differentiation of subject matter between biology and psychology. Indeed, the growing approach of biological psychology is given a special privilege and considered to be the gold standard school of psychology. The identification of psychological life and the brain is never critically evaluated despite an extreme emphasis on critical thinking, which instead challenges human experience and science that falls short of the ideals of experimental methodology. The study of psychological phenomena by means of neuroscience is a prominent if not the preeminent aspirational goal of the entire discipline. The very existence of any psychological phenomenon is viewed as most strongly supported when neuroscience is able to identify its manifestation in the brain. In other words, although psychological processes are investigated in research throughout psychology, these studies are part of a scientific project whose ultimate aim and promise is to explain them neurologically.

There is a connection between the two unquestioned philosophical assumptions of scientism: the metaphysical physicalism and the epistemological positivism. Even though psychological processes are researched and theorized as such, the methodological orthodoxy requiring causal hypothesis, operational definition of variables, statistical analyses, and causal inference already treats mental life as if it were a physical thing that could be objectified, manipulated, measured, and quantitatively analyzed. Phenomenological philosophers have shown how the ontological and epistemological assumptions involved here are unified in the uncritically assumed position of naturalism (Husserl, 1954), which continues to pervade the way psychology is introduced and taught. From this it follows that even as genuine psychology has been emerging in our discipline over its history, the methodological tyranny of scientism drives the discipline toward a naturalization of psychological phenomena that prepares the way for eventual biological reductionism, hence increasingly prominent and encroaching status of biological psychology.

Perhaps most prominent in the Lilienfeld et al. (2018) text, however, is the aspect of scientism that dogmatically places (an erroneously narrowed view of) science above all human experience and expertise in everyday life, the professions, and even in science itself to the extent that they do not achieve the gold standard of causal explanations supported by true experiments. In other words, human experience and all forms of human knowledge is viewed as flawed, illusory, and in need of edification by science, which stands alone as the only legitimate form of human reason. Indeed, every chapter of the text features multiple pages denouncing various kinds of pseudoscience and reiterating deficiency vis-à-vis evidence of causality supported by experimental research design. The text relentlessly emphasizes 'critical thinking', but all critical thinking is directed to the nonscientific, the pseudoscientific, the deficiently scientific, and the preliminary stages of science; there is no critical thinking about science itself or about the aspiration toward causal explanation and physical reduction as the gold standard and only true source of human knowledge. There is no critique of science from any other standpoint, for instance those of public intellectuals, religious leaders, or representatives of non-Westernized cultures, even though a huge literature supports such critiques. No credit is given to philosophy, anthropology, theology, or any discipline except to the extent that it adheres to the orthodoxy of scientism. This pervasive, dogmatic, and fundamentally philosophical orientation, radically lacking in philosophical sophistication, betrays the central project of this text as propaganda for a flawed ideology masquerading as science. This is all the more astonishing in light of the authors' explicit claim not to be addressing metaphysical questions and admission that science is incapable of doing so (Lilienfeld et al., 2018, p. 12). Gantt's observation in this volume that the dogma of scientism is itself not amenable to scientific test applies here, revealing the faulty foundation—call it the *dishonesty*—of the overarching project embodied in this introduction to psychology.

The analyses presented in this volume therefore have an important place in our developing field, and much work remains if psychology is to become liberated from scientism. The struggle has been underway since the very inception of psychology and has yielded fruits, as we have seen, by those who clearly see the problem and also by those whose intuitive grasp of psychological subject matter enable them to move the discipline toward genuine science even with inadequate methods and theories. This struggle is likely to continue. At stake is the very saving of mental life as a reality to be known and the success of a universal science that is genuinely capable of providing knowledge of all, not just material existence. Beyond science, also at stake is a humanity that understands itself in all its gifts, which include not only science but many other kinds of expertise ranging from the professions to intellectual, religious, and political leadership, each of which is, together with and in no way inferior to science, crucial in the self-determining destiny of humankind, on which the natural and living world also depends.

Notes

1 See Osbeck (in press) for an explication of shared dimensions and mutually informative contributions of various disciplines, including natural sciences, human sciences, humanities, and the arts.
2 "[M]an as we know him, for better or worse, is what man has made of man" (Skinner, 1971, p. 206). To the question of whether in operant conditioning the person is "merely a victim or passive" of an external causality, Skinner answers, "He is indeed controlled by his environment, but we must remember that it is an environment that is largely of his own making. The evolution of culture is a gigantic exercise in self-control" (1971, p. 215).
3 For the generative dialogue in neuroscience and cognitive science with phenomenology, see Di Paolo and De Jaegher (2012) and Stewart, Gapenne, and Di Paolo (2010).
4 Qualitative methods and methodology are featured in the APA journal *Qualitative Psychology*, which institutes norms for scientific research that are both authentically psychological and integrative.

References

Allport, G. W. (1942). *The use of personal documents in psychological science*. Prepared for the Committee on the Appraisal of Research, Bulletin #49. New York: Social Science Council.

Atwood, G. E., & Stolorow, R. D. (1984). *Structures of subjectivity: Explorations in psychoanalytic phenomenology and contextualism*. New York: Routledge.

Bandura, A. (1977). *Social learning theory*. Oxford: Prentice-Hall.

Baerveldt, C., & Verheggen, T. (1999). Enactivism and the experiential reality of culture: Rethinking the epistemological basis of cultural psychology. *Culture & Psychology*, 5(2), 183–206.

Brentano, F. (1973). *Psychology from an empirical standpoint* (A. C. Rancurello, D. B. Terrell, & L. L. McAlister, Trans.). New York: Humanities Press. (Original work published 1874)

Creswell, J. W., Klassen, A. C., Piano Clark, V. L., & Clegg Smith, K. (2011). *Best practices for mixed methods research in the health sciences*. Washington, DC: Office of Behavioral and Social Science Research, National Institutes of Health.

Dilthey, W. (1977). Ideas concerning a descriptive and analytical psychology. In W. Dilthey (Ed.), *Descriptive psychology and historical understanding* (R. M. Zaner & K. L. Heiges, Trans.). The Hague: Martinus Nijhoff. (Original work published 1894)

Di Paolo, E., & De Jaegher, H. (2012). The interactive brain hypothesis. *Frontiers in Human Neuroscience*, 7(6), Article ID163.

Flanagan, J. C. (1954). The critical incident technique. *Psychological Bulletin*, 51(4), 327–358.

Freeman, M., & Wertz, F. (2012). Qualitative inquiry joins the division: Beginning the dialogue. *Score: APA Division of Evaluation, Statistics and Measurement Newsletter*, 34(3), 5–7. Retrieved from www.apa.org/divisions/div5/pdf/July12Score.pdf

Freud, S. (1977). A project for scientific psychology (unfinished manuscript). In *The origins of psychoanalysis: Letters to Wilhelm Fliess, drafts, and notes:*

1887–1902 (pp. 345–445). New York: Basic Books. (Original work published 1895)

Giorgi, A. (1970). *Psychology as a human science*. New York: Harper and Row.

Guntrip, H. (1971). *Psychoanalytic theory, therapy, and the self*. New York: Basic Books.

Hall, R., & Nemirovsky, R. (2012). Introduction to the special issue: Modalities of Engagement in Mathematical Activity and Learning. *Journal of the Learning Sciences, 21*, 207–215.

Husserl, E. 1954. *The crisis of European sciences and transcendental phenomenology* (D. Carr, Trans.). Evanston, IL: Northwestern University Press.

Lilienfeld, S.O., Lynn, S.J., & Namy, L.L. (2018). *Psychology: From inquiry to understanding*. New York: Pearson.

McGann, M., De Jaegher, H., & Di Paolo, E. (2013). Enaction and psychology. *Review of General Psychology, 17*(2), 203–209.

Mitchell, S.A., & Aron, L. (1999). *Relational psychoanalysis: The emergence of a tradition*. Hillsdale, NJ: Analytic Press.

Osbeck, L.M. (in press). *Values in psychological science: Reimagining epistemic priorities*. Cambridge: Cambridge University Press.

Osbeck, L.M., & Held, B. (2014). *Rational intuition: Philosophical roots, scientific investigations*. Cambridge: Cambridge University Press.

Osbeck, L.M., Nersessian, N.J., Malone, K.R., & Newstetter, W.C. (2011). *Science as psychology: Sense making and identity in science practice*. Cambridge: Cambridge University Press.

Rotter, J. (1954). *Social learning and clinical psychology*. Englewood Cliffs, NJ: Prentice-Hall.

Skinner, B.F. (1971). *Beyond freedom and dignity*. New York: Alfred A. Knopf.

Stewart, J., Gapenne, O., & Di Paolo, E.A. (Eds.). (2010). *Enaction: Towards a new paradigm of cognitive science*. Cambridge, MA: MIT Press.

Watson, J.B. (1925). *Behaviorism*. New York: W.W. Norton.

Wertz, F.J. (1998). The role of the humanistic movement in the history of psychology. *Journal of Humanistic Psychology, 38*(1), 42–70.

Wertz, F.J. (2006). Phenomenological currents in 20th century psychology. In H. Dreyfus & M.A. Wrathall (Eds.), *Companion to existential-phenomenological philosophy* (pp. 392–408). Oxford: Blackwell.

Wertz, F.J. (2011). The qualitative revolution and psychology: Science, politics, and ethics. *Humanistic Psychologist, 39*, 77–104.

Wertz, F.J. (2014). Qualitative inquiry in the history of psychology. *Qualitative Psychology, 1*, 4–16.

Wertz, F.J., & Olbert, C. (2016). The convergence of Freud's psychoanalysis and Husserl's phenomenology on a research approach for human sciences. In C. Fischer, L. Laubscher, & R. Brooke (Eds.), *The qualitative vision in psychology: Invitation to a human science approach* (pp. 244–269). Pittsburgh, PA: Duquesne University Press.

Index

Printed in the United States
by Baker & Taylor Publisher Services

Printed in the United States
by Baker & Taylor Publisher Services